# THE JUMBO BOOK OF OUTDOOR ART

Kids Can Press acknowledges the financial support of the Government of Ontario, through the Ontario Media Development Corporation's Ontario Book Initiative; the Ontario Arts Council; the Canada Council for the Arts; and the Government of Canada, through the BPIDP, for our publishing activity.

| | |
|---|---|
| Published in Canada by | Published in the U.S. by |
| Kids Can Press Ltd. | Kids Can Press Ltd. |
| 29 Birch Avenue | 2250 Military Road |
| Toronto, ON  M4V 1E2 | Tonawanda, NY  14150 |

www.kidscanpress.com

Edited by Stacey Roderick
Designed by Julia Naimska
Photography by Ray Boudreau and Doug Hall
Printed and bound in China

This book is limp sewn with drawn-on cover.

CM PA 06 0 9 8 7 6 5 4 3 2 1

**National Library of Canada Cataloguing in Publication Data**

Luxbacher, Irene, 1970–
    The jumbo book of outdoor art / written and illustrated by Irene Luxbacher.
Includes index.

On cover: An artistic adventure from the Avenue Road Arts School.

ISBN-13: 978-1-55337-680-4
ISBN-10: 1-55337-680-3

1. Art—Technique—Juvenile literature.  2. Nature in art—Juvenile literature.
3. Nature (Aesthetics)—Juvenile literature.  I. Title.

N7440.L893 2006     j704.9'43     C2005-907020-X

Kids Can Press is a ℓ𝒪ℝ𝒰𝒮™ Entertainment company

## Dedication

*To the amazing staff, artists and instructors at the Avenue Road Arts School, whose hard work and dedication continue to make a difference. And to all the artistic adventurers out there who dare to dream.*

## Acknowledgments

Many thanks to the following artists/instructors for their imaginative and thoughtful ideas: Jennifer Chin, Taggett Cornish, Liana Del Mastro Vicente, Madeleine Dominigue, Julie Frost, Julie Galloway, Martha Johnson, Joni Moriyama, Linda Prussick, Julianne Trewartha and Susie Whaley. Special thanks also to Lola Rasminsky, Director of the Avenue Road Arts School, for her remarkable vision, effort and support of arts education. Also, thanks to Kids Can Press for their encouragement, support and expertise, particularly Valerie Hussey, Stacey Roderick, Julia Naimska and Rachel Di Salle. Thanks also to Ray Boudreau and Doug Hall for their wonderful photography.

A portion of the proceeds from the sale of this book will be used to support the activities of Arts for Children of Toronto, a registered charity associated with the Avenue Road Arts School. Through scholarship and outreach programs, Arts for Children of Toronto provides high quality arts experiences to thousands of children who might not otherwise enjoy these opportunities. For more information about the Avenue Road Arts School, please visit www.avenueroadartsschool.com.

An artistic adventure from the
Avenue Road Arts School

KIDS • CAN • PRESS

The JUMBO
BOOK OF
OUTDOOR
ART

Written and illustrated by
Irene Luxbacher

KIDS CAN PRESS

# enTs

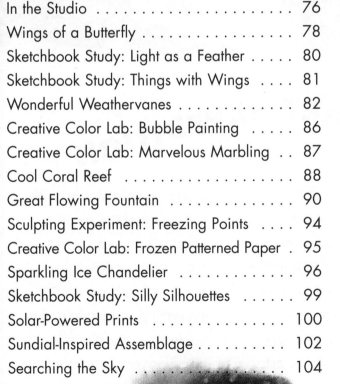

ook out! You could be standing in the middle of your next artistic adventure! The next time you go for a walk outside, take a look at what's underfoot and overhead. Inspirational scenery and magical materials are all around you. Earth, grass, leaves, flowers, bugs, trees, birds, wind, sun and water are just a few sources of inspiration for your natural creativity.

# A GREAT OUTDOOR ART EXPEDITION

At the Avenue Road Arts School, we believe art is a wild adventure. So, come with us and explore all that nature has to offer while you draw out your best ideas, paint colorful creations and sculpt 3-dimensional works of art. Precious metal masterpieces, incredible creepy crawlers, wonderful weathervanes and amazing animal masks are just a few of the exciting creations you can make. From deep underground to the stars above and everything in between, the outdoors is the place to discover your artistic talents.

Here are a few Avenue Road tips to get your ideas growing.

## ● Start a collection

Use your artist's eye to collect natural materials you like the look, feel or even the smell of. Keep them in a special place, such as a box or treasure chest, and add something new every time you go to the park, into your backyard, to the beach or to the woods.

Sniff, sniff. Mmm ... I'm definitely keeping this!

## ● Respect your environment

Never hurt or damage plants or creatures when you are adding to your collection of naturally fun finds. Try recycling old or used materials, too. And always ask permission before taking anything from someone else's property.

## ● Be brave

Don't be afraid to try out new tools, techniques or materials that seem unusual. Also, if you don't have something we suggest, look around and use something you do have instead. Amazing artistic discoveries are made when you're willing to try something new.

## ● Stay safe

Make sure you always have an adult along for the trip when your ideas lead you outdoors. If you have an allergy to any of the materials in the list of Artist's Tools (for example, grass or pollen from flowers), try something else you like the look of. Always read labels to make sure supplies are nontoxic and so

Excuse me. I need some help, please.

that you understand the instructions. Also, be very careful using adult tools, such as glue guns. When in doubt, get help from an older art adventurer.

## ● Have fun

This is the most important tip. Having fun is the best way to make sure your artistic expeditions are a success. When you are having fun, there are no mistakes — only exciting artful ideas to try!

Let's go!

So get ready: the great outdoors is calling. For an artistic adventurer, there's nothing more exciting than taking a walk on the wild side!

# Digging deep

The earth under our feet is a gold mine of groundbreaking ideas.

**Earthenware Extravaganza** (page 14)

**Precious Metal Masterpiece** (page 24)

**Prehistoric Painting** (page 32)

**Layered Landscape**
(page 12)

**Regal Gems and Jewels**
(page 18)

**Dinosaur Graveyard**
(page 34)

# In the Studio

Here are some tools and materials you can use
for your earthy explorations.

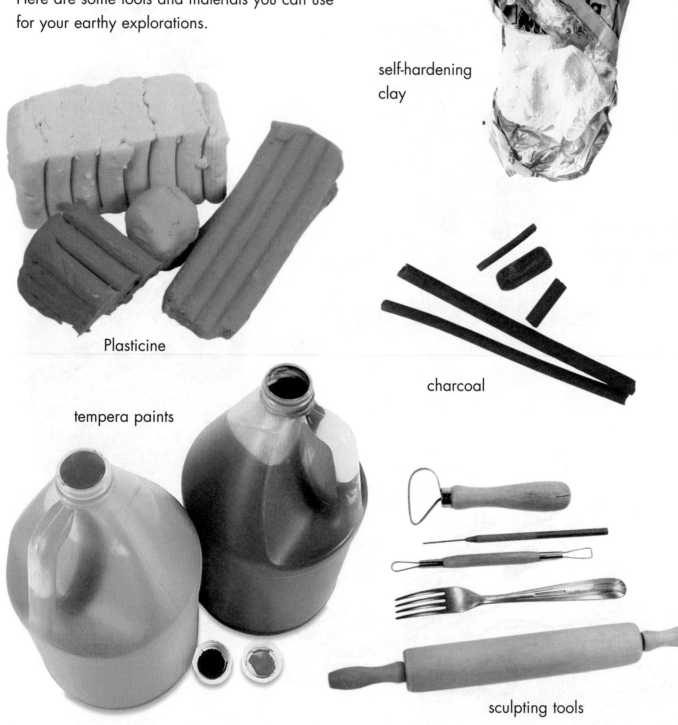

self-hardening
clay

Plasticine

charcoal

tempera paints

sculpting tools

acrylic paints

paintbrushes

gravel

sand

trowel

soil

rocks, stones and pebbles

• Whatever you can't collect from the outdoors, you can find in art supply and craft stores, hardware stores, pet stores or aquarium shops and home decorating stores.

# A LAYERED LANDSCAPE

If you could take an elevator down to the center of the earth, you would pass through lots of different layers. Make a sculpture of what you might find if you dug down through the earth's crust.

## Artist's Tools

- wide-mouthed clear jar or container
- newspapers
- collection of layering materials (soil, pebbles, marbles, sand gravel, clay, Plasticine, florist's foam, gold glitter, etc.)
- spoon
- fun finds (sticks, twigs, moss, old toys, etc.)
- self-hardening clay and fine wire (optional)
- acrylic paints or permanent markers
- paintbrush

**1** Place your jar on top of the newspapers and gather an assortment of earthy-looking samples into small piles.

**2** Choose one of your samples and pour or scoop it into your jar. Use your hand or spoon to spread your sample out evenly.

**3** Continue layering your different earthy samples until you run out or your jar is filled. Choose layers that are different colors and textures.

**4** Use some fun finds to create a miniature scene on top of the last layer. Try adding

- small clay figures or plastic toys

- tiny stars made from fine wire and modeling clay

- miniature trees made from twigs and moss

- mini mountains made from stones or small rocks

**5** For a finishing touch, add some lava-like layers and cool creatures to the outside of the jar with acrylic paints or permanent markers.

## Rock Research

Before starting a project, artists often research the materials or theme they're exploring. Check out a book on geology (the study of rocks and earth) to learn more about the earth's layers. It might inspire some interesting ideas for your Layered Landscape.

# EARTHENWARE EXTRAVAGANZA

Clay is a type of soil that artists through the ages have been using to create cups, plates and containers called earthenware. What kind of earthenware will you create? A fairy teacup? A royal goblet? A s-s-super urn?

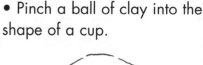

## Artist's Tools

- cloth or canvas to cover work surface
- self-hardening clay (natural or colored)
- rolling pin
- sculpting tools (string, fork, plastic knife, stick, pencil, etc.)
- fun finds (leaves, beads, twigs, wire, aluminum foil, etc.)
- acrylic paints
- damp cloth or fine brush

**1** Start by making a simple container using one of these methods:

- Roll pieces of clay into long snakey pieces and coil them into the shape of a vase or urn. Be careful not to make your coils too thin or they might break.

- Pinch a ball of clay into the shape of a cup.

- Flatten a piece of clay with your hands or rolling pin and place it over a round object such as a ball or crumpled up newspaper to make a bowl shape.

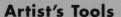

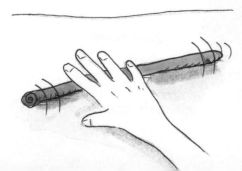

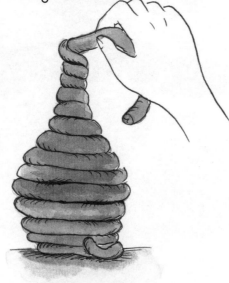

**2** Before your clay dries, roll, press and cut out smaller bits of clay for added details like a base or a handle. Pinch, press and smooth your pieces together so they don't fall off when they dry.

**3** Carve or cut in designs and decoration with your sculpting tools.

**4** Press, poke or pinch in some fun finds as decoration.

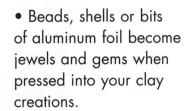

• Beads, shells or bits of aluminum foil become jewels and gems when pressed into your clay creations.

• Use a stick or wire coil for a lovely stem to turn a bowl or cup into a gorgeous goblet.

**5** After letting your earthenware dry, use a damp cloth to dab on larger areas of acrylic paint or a fine brush to paint on delicate details.

## Artist's Tip

Artists often use the term "organic forms" to describe shapes that are free flowing or look like things you find in nature, such as plants or animals.

# OGRES, GNOMES AND TERRIBLE TROLLS

Dig deep into your imagination and use some clay to create cool creatures that might live far below ground level.

## Artist's Tools

- cloth or canvas to cover work surface
- self-hardening clay
- rolling pin
- garlic press
- sculpting tools (string, fork, plastic knife, stick, pencil, etc.)
- fun finds (beads, shells, stones, leaves, twigs, etc.)
- acrylic paints and paintbrushes

**1** Mold some clay into a fun form for your figure's body. What shape will your clay creature be? Pear-shaped? Round? Oval?

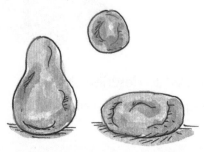

**2** Roll out some round balls and snakes in the palms of your hands to make arms, legs and a head or two. Pinch, press and smooth your pieces together well so they don't fall off as they dry.

**3** Press out a few flat pancakes with your hands or rolling pin. Thicker pieces can make a base for your figure to stand on. Very thin, flat pieces can be cut and wrapped around your figure for cool clothing.

**4** Squeeze some clay through your garlic press to add some hair or a long beard.

**5** Pinch, poke and scratch to add texture and delightful details such as facial features to a surface.

**6** Carve or cut in a few finishing touches.

**7** Press in a few fun finds to add more character to your creation.

**8** Let your clay creature dry.

**9** Brush on a light coat of acrylic paint or leave your creature unpainted and rough looking.

## In a Muddle?

You don't always need store-bought clay to have a little sculpting fun. The next time you're in a garden or a space you're allowed to dig, see what kinds of silly sculptures you can create with the earth, soil, sand or clay you dig up.

# REGAL GEMS AND JEWELS

Use your sculpting know-how to transform rocks and pebbles into gems and jewelry fit for real royalty!

## Artist's Tools

- collection of rocks and pebbles
- magnifying glass (if you have one)
- rag and store-bought or homemade vegetable dyes (see page 53)
- white glue, paintbrush and glitter
- clear nail polish or varnish
- aluminum foil or metal foil*
- scissors
- 20-gauge wire
- fine needlenose pliers
- string or long stick

* Metal foil is a bit stronger than aluminum foil. It is easy to work with and can be found in art supply stores and craft shops.

**1** Use your artistic eye to choose some favorite stones or pebbles with interesting colors, shapes, sizes or textures. A magnifying glass will help you see small details such as impressions, fossils or tiny sparkling flecks. The closer you look, the more you'll see.

**2** Turn your collection of stones into gemlike jewels.

• Rub a rag dipped in vegetable dye over some of your stones. Try sapphire-blue, ruby-red or emerald-green stains.

• Brush a bit of white glue and sprinkle a little glitter onto dyed or plain stones or pebbles.

• Add dots of clear nail polish or varnish to give any small stone more sparkle and shine.

**3** Create some sparkling settings (the part of a piece of jewelry that holds a gem in place).

• Scrunch a piece of aluminum foil or bend a square of metal foil into a nest that fits snugly around your stone. Hold the stone in place with a dab of glue.

• Wrap a thin piece of wire around your stone or gem. Use more wire to create a web of patterns and designs that surround your stone. Needlenose pliers will help you bend your wire into intricate patterns.

**4** Turn your gorgeous gems into royal accessories.

• Slip string through the setting of a medium-sized jewel to make a majestic medallion.

• Use wire to attach a larger gem or jewel to a stick to make a great royal scepter.

Turn the page to find out how to make the perfect crown for your regal gems and jewels.

# Crowning Touch

## Artist's Tools

- cardboard or bristol board
- scissors
- gold acrylic paint or white glue and gold glitter
- ribbon
- gold or silver metallic markers
- regal gems and jewels or gemlike beads
- glue gun and gloves

**1** Cut a piece of cardboard or bristol board that is long enough to fit around your head. Draw and cut out a zigzag pattern across the top.

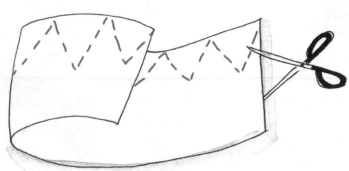

**2** Paint your cardboard crown with gold acrylic paints, or brush on some white glue and sprinkle with golden glitter. Let dry.

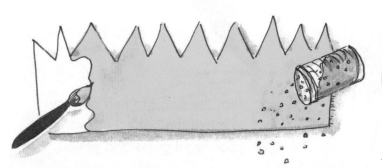

**3** With an adult's help, poke holes in both ends of the cardboard. Tie the ends together with ribbon at the back.

**4** Add some decorative details with metallic markers or more glitter.

**5** With an adult's help, attach your gems and jewels with the glue gun.

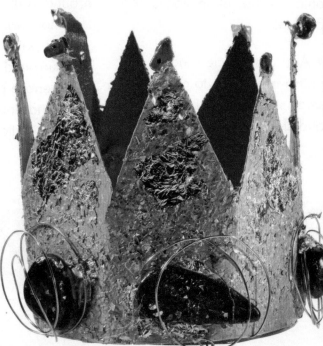

# A Precious Princess's Crown

## Artist's Tools

- fine wire
- regal gems and jewels or gemlike beads
- fun finds (aluminum foil, dried flowers, feathers, etc.)
- white glue

**1** Twist and twirl the wire into a delicate garland or crown.

**2** Beads and gems can be tied on with more wire. Delicate decorations like triangles of aluminum foil and dried flowers can be glued on, too.

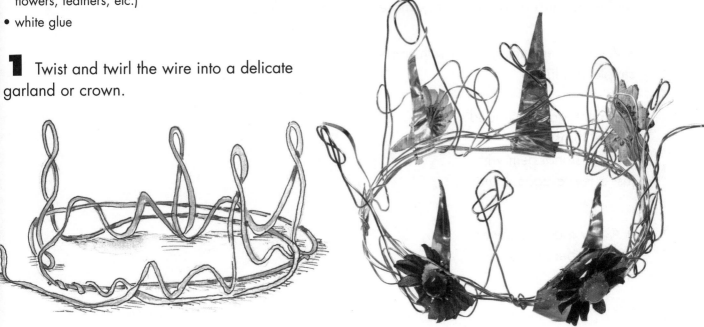

# Ocean Inspired

A twisted length of aluminum foil and some seashells can be the start of a cool crown fit for the royalty of an underwater world!

# Dramatic Designs

You can turn some simple flat shapes into 3-dimensional gems and jewels just by adding a few more lines and shading.

• A circle becomes a pearl with some simple shading.

• A pentagon (a 5-sided shape) turns into a 3-dimensional gem with just a few diagonal lines.

• A few triangles joined together become a diamond.

• A rectangle becomes a chest for your drawn treasures.

# Scratching the Surface

Here's how to turn acrylic paint colors into beautiful gem tones.

**1** Brush a light coat of your favorite color of acrylic paint onto the shiny side of a piece of heavy bristol board or foam core.

**2** While the paint is wet, use a paper towel or clean rag to gently wipe or rub a simple shape into the paint. Let dry.

**3** Spray your painted surface with a little water and use your rag or paper towel to gently wipe off the watermarks.

**4** Repeat steps 1 through 3, layering different paint colors. Let dry.

**5** Use a white chalk pastel or the tip of your brush handle to add delicate lines to your gem of a painting.

# PRECIOUS METAL MASTERPIECE

This is a painting project you can fill with rich, earthy ideas.

## Artist's Tools

- containers for paints
- acrylic paints
- paintbrushes, regular and 2 with soft bristles
- large piece of bristol board or foam core
- paper towels or clean rag
- spray bottle and water
- gold size and fake silver or gold leaf*
- chalk pastels or fine markers

\* Silver or gold leaf and gold size are easy to find in art supply stores and safe to use. Gold leaf might be a bit tricky to work with at first, so you might want some help from an adult art adventurer.

**1** In separate plastic containers, mix a very tiny drop of brown paint into a few other colors such as green, yellow, orange, purple, red or blue.

**2** Choose one of your mixed paints and add a little water to thin it out. With a regular paintbrush, brush this mixture over your bristol board or foam core, covering it completely.

**4** Lightly spray your wet, painted surface with water. Gently blot or rub the paint again with a rag or paper towel, leaving earthy marks that look like pebbles, sand and stones. Let dry.

**3** While the paint is wet, use a paper towel or rag to gently wipe some soft, simple shapes onto your painted surface. Try to make shapes that remind you of creatures and rock formations you might find deep down underground.

**5** Repeat steps 2 to 4 using a different color of paint for each layer.

**6** Dip a soft paintbrush in the gold size and brush it over a few of your earthy shapes. Let the size dry until it is clear and sticky to the touch.

**7** Carefully place small pieces or squares of gold or silver leaf over the parts of your picture that are sticky with gold size. Gently pat them down with your finger.

**8** Use a dry, soft brush to brush off any of the gold or silver leaf that didn't stick.

**9** Add the finishing touches.

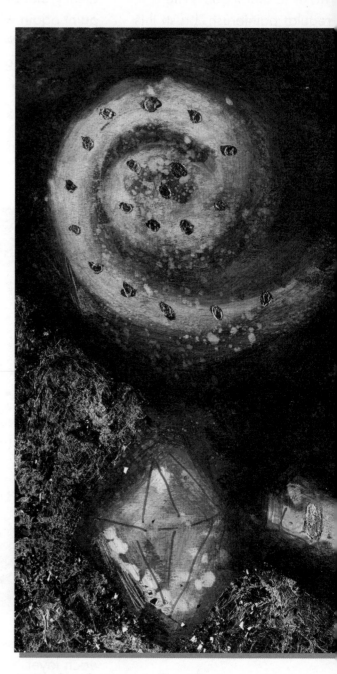

• specks of pure acrylic color

• soft chalk pastel smudges

• fine marker lines

# CAVERNOUS CREATION

Use your imagination to create a hidden landscape of deep, dark caves and caverns.

## Artist's Tools

- newsprint or gray pastel paper
- pencil and eraser
- charcoal or black conte
- white chalk or white conte
- black and white acrylic inks
- watercolor paintbrushes

**1** On the newsprint or pastel paper, lightly sketch a creepy, cavelike scene with your pencil. Be sure to include things like

- stalactites (stone formations that hang from the roof of a cave and look like icicles)

- bumpy boulders

- hanging and flying bats

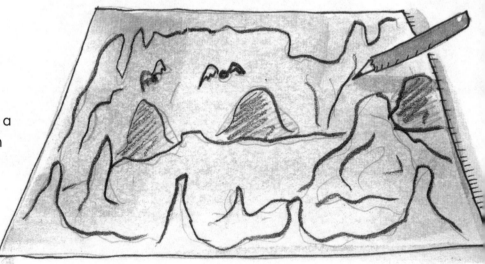

- stalagmites (stone formations that grow up from the floor of a cave and look like upside-down icicles)

- caves and caverns

**2** Use charcoal or black conte to add shadows to the parts of your picture you want to look deep and dark.

**3** Use white chalk or conte to add highlights to the parts of your picture you want to look light and easy to see.

**4** Use the eraser or your finger to smudge some of your highlights and shadows together to create softer gray tones. This will help your scene look a little more realistic.

**5** Paint in the parts of your picture that you want to look pitch black with the black acrylic ink.

**6** Paint in the parts of your picture that need tiny highlighted details with the white ink.

# Earthy Tones

Did you know you can make paints from soil samples? Different types of soil contain pigments, or colors, for making a palette of interesting earth tones.

**1** Collect your soil samples in separate jars or containers.

• Dense, heavy clay from the garden can be red, gray or yellow.

• Sandy soil is beige or light brown.

• Potting soil can be deep, dark brown or black.

**2** Use a rock or thick stick to crush and grind your earth samples into a powder or paste.

**3** Add a small amount of lard, vegetable oil or shortening and stir it thoroughly until the mixture is smooth and easy to spread.

**4** Try mixing a few of your mixed samples together with a brush or palette knife to create even more colors.

**5** Store your paints in a closed, labeled container and in a cool, dry place such as the refrigerator so they don't dry out or go bad.

# Soil Smudges

**1** Sprinkle a little dry earth or soil on your page.

**2** Use your finger or an eraser to smudge and spread your sprinkles of earth into some simple shapes.

**3** Use a fine brush or ink pen to add details such as eyes, whiskers or a tail to your smudged shapes.

# Artist's Tip

You can use charcoal instead of soil samples.

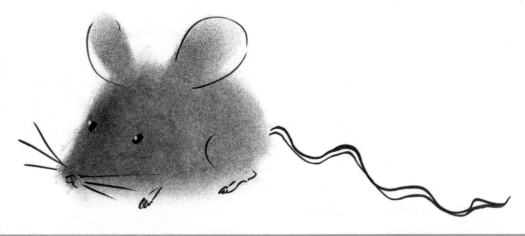

# PREHISTORIC PAINTING

Try some of these techniques for a cave painting that will take you way back in time.

### Artist's Tools

- collection of flat stones and rocks
- newspaper
- homemade paints (see page 30) or powdered tempera paints
- containers for paints and water
- paintbrushes, thick and thin
- chalk or charcoal
- chalk pastels

**1** Clean your rocks with water. Let dry on a newspaper-covered work surface.

**2** While your rocks dry, prepare your homemade paints or mix up some powdered tempera paints. Adding lots of water to the tempera will make your paint thin and transparent. Adding only a little water will make your paint thick and opaque.

**3** Look at the shapes of your stones. Do they remind you of anything? A funny face? An ancient animal? An interesting scene?

**4** Sketch some simple shapes and forms onto your rocks using a piece of chalk or charcoal.

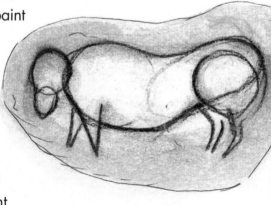

**5** Add some rich, earthy colors to your drawings with paints and a thick brush or rub on chalk pastels with your fingers.

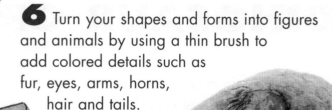

**6** Turn your shapes and forms into figures and animals by using a thin brush to add colored details such as fur, eyes, arms, horns, hair and tails.

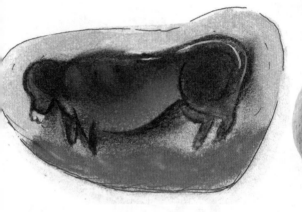

## Artful Idea

Paint lots of little scenes on smaller rocks, and put your scenes together to tell a story. Or paint all your images or scenes on one big, flat rock.

## Ancient Art

The most famous cave painting ever discovered is in Lascaux, France, and is believed to have been painted around 17 000 years ago!

# DINOSAUR GRAVEYARD

Go on an archaeological dig and unearth some cool stone shapes. They're perfect for piecing together the parts of a dinosaur.

## Artist's Tools

- collection of rocks, stones and pebbles
- patch of earth or shallow box filled with sand or soil
- dry tempera paints (optional)
- self-hardening clay
- black and white chalk pastels

**1** Examine your collection of rocks, stones and pebbles. Let the shapes, sizes, colors and textures inspire some ideas. Which rocks remind you of

- funny feet
- huge heads
- long legs
- big bodies

**2** Lay the stone bones out in a prehistoric shape on the ground or in a shallow box filled with sand or soil. (By adding dry tempera paint powders to the soil or sand, you can create a dry but colorful background for your dinosaur bones.)

**3** Roll and pinch bits of clay to make any bonelike shapes that might be missing from your dinosaur.

**4** Add some embellishments.

• Black chalk pastel can be rubbed over the parts of your bones you want to stand out.

• White chalk pastel can be rubbed over the bones so they look like they're all from the same skeletal structure.

# Extinct Images

Use a stick and some stones to create a large-scale dinosaur drawing in a stretch of sand or soil. Take a photo of your giant dinosaur drawing. In time, your drawing will wash or blow away, but your photo will be a souvenir of the extinct image.

# Quick Sand Studies

Sand is a terrific material for building temporary sculptures. Next time you're at the beach or in a sandbox, try these techniques and make spectacular sand sculptures.

Start with sand just wet enough to hold its shape when you squeeze it in your hands. Keep a spray bottle or watering can handy to moisten your sand while you work.

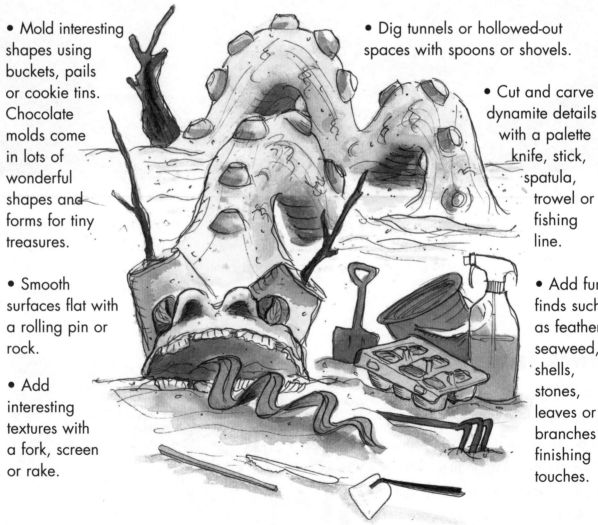

• Mold interesting shapes using buckets, pails or cookie tins. Chocolate molds come in lots of wonderful shapes and forms for tiny treasures.

• Smooth surfaces flat with a rolling pin or rock.

• Add interesting textures with a fork, screen or rake.

• Dig tunnels or hollowed-out spaces with spoons or shovels.

• Cut and carve dynamite details with a palette knife, stick, spatula, trowel or fishing line.

• Add fun finds such as feathers, seaweed, shells, stones, leaves or branches for finishing touches.

# Sticky Situation

By mixing sand with white glue and water you can create some cool, longer-lasting sand sculptures.

**1** Pour 125 mL (1/2 cup) of white glue into a bucket or plastic container.

**2** Add 250 mL (1 cup) of water to your glue and stir.

**3** Pour in a handful of sand at a time, mixing it with a stick or old spoon. Add sand until you have a thick sand mixture that's not too runny (too much water) or too dry (too much sand). If you like, mix in some buried treasures like small pebbles, marbles or shells.

**4** Use an old spoon or spatula to scoop, spread and mold your sticky sand into silly sculptures or cool rock formations. Let dry.

# UNDERGROUND KINGDOM

What would you find if you uncovered an ancient underground kingdom?

## Artist's Tools

- shallow box lined with plastic garbage bag
- sculpting screen (found in art supply stores)
- scissors and work gloves
- sand
- bucket
- white glue
- water
- mixing spoon or stick
- self-hardening clay
- Plasticine
- carving tools (plastic knife, fork, nail file, etc.)
- decorating materials (gold glitter, sea salt, aluminum foil, etc.)
- fun finds (twigs, bark, moss, beads, roots, stones, etc.)

## Make a Terrain

**1** Wearing work gloves, fill your plastic-lined box with a length of your sculpting screen or mesh. Try shaping your screen into

- pointed peaks
- deep valleys
- creepy caverns

**2** Follow the instructions on page 37 to make a batch of sand-and-glue mixture.

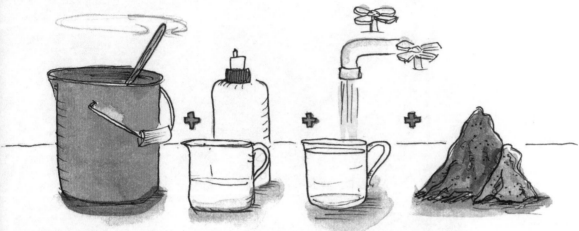

**3** Working on a small section at a time, scoop and press your sticky sand mixture onto your sculpted screen until it is completely covered.

**4** Drizzle and smoothe a little white glue over the sand-covered screen. Set your sandy terrain aside to dry overnight.

**5** Simple structures to make up your underground scene could be

• a creepy castle made of self-hardening clay and small stones

• Plasticine troll houses glued to flat stone landings

• rocky formations such as clay stalactites and stalagmites (sprinkle some salt over your forms to give them a crystal-like appearance)

• a rushing underground river and deep pool made out of painted Plasticine

**6** Add the finishing touches to your ancient underground kingdom.

• Populate your kingdom with ogres, gnomes and terrible trolls (see page 16).

• Use acrylic paint to add mysterious doorways and wall paintings.

• Use glue or clay to attach stones, rocks or pebbles to buildings, roads or walls.

• Rickety ladders made from dried twigs and spooky stairs molded out of self-hardening clay make great troll pathways.

• Use fun finds such as twigs, dried roots, bark and moss to add earthy details.

# Going Green

Fantastic foliage, awesome organics and interesting insects are the seeds of great green ideas!

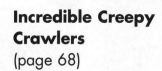

**Incredible Creepy Crawlers**
(page 68)

**Terrific Topiaries**
(page 50)

**Beautiful Batik** (page 54)

**Soft Snake Sculpture**
(page 56)

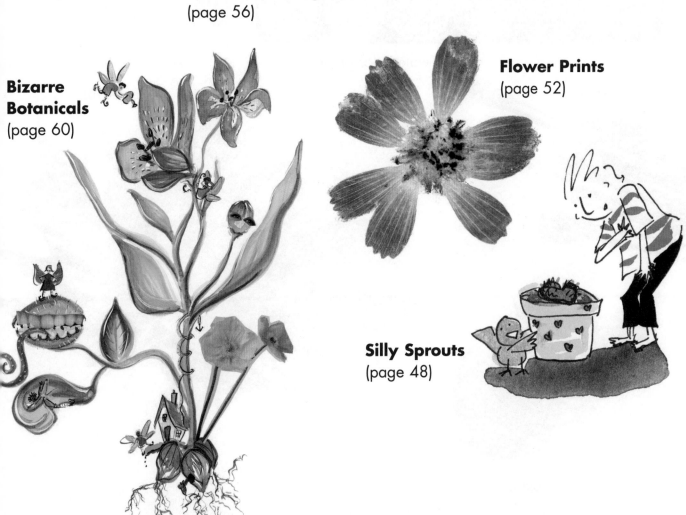

**Bizarre Botanicals**
(page 60)

**Flower Prints**
(page 52)

**Silly Sprouts**
(page 48)

# In the Studio

Some tools and materials you can
use for going a little wild.

paint palette

watercolor paints

paintbrushes

leaves

bulbs

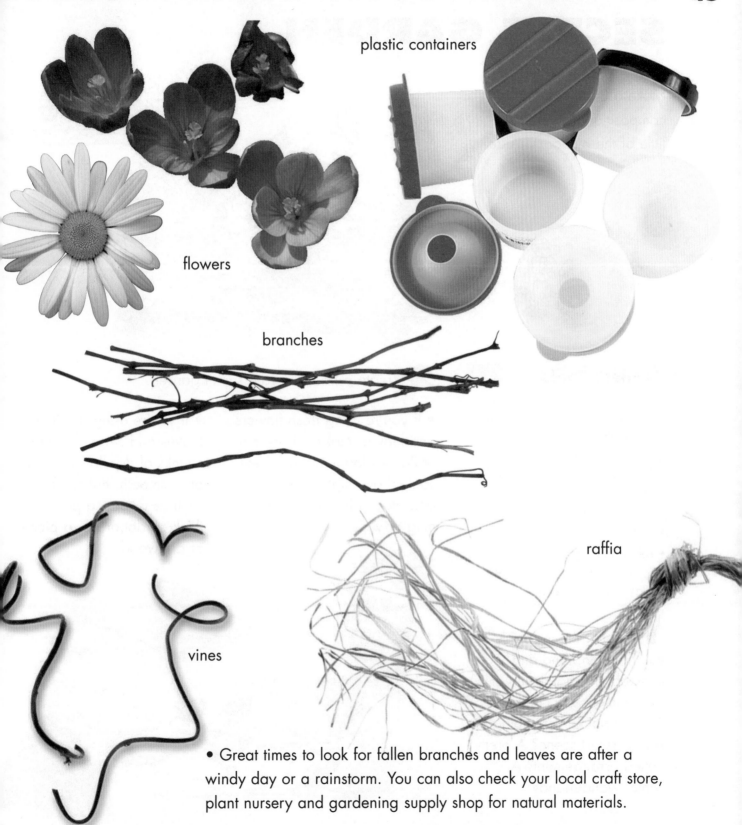

plastic containers

flowers

branches

raffia

vines

• Great times to look for fallen branches and leaves are after a windy day or a rainstorm. You can also check your local craft store, plant nursery and gardening supply shop for natural materials.

# SECRET GARDEN

Make a 3-dimensional composition that brings a little of the outdoors inside.

## Artist's Tools

- samples of seasonal foliage (leaves, grass, branches, flowers, vines, etc.)
- container or base (basket, flowerpot, flat rock, driftwood, etc.)
- florist's foam
- water
- self-hardening clay
- fun finds (shells, stones, feathers, plastic animals, etc.)

**1** Lay out the materials you have on hand and think about what theme or environment you can make. A lush tropical assemblage? A dry desert scene? A pretty potted arrangement? A winter wonderland?

**2** Create a base for your secret garden.

• If you're using fresh flowers and leaves, make a base out of florist's foam that has been soaked overnight in water and placed in a flowerpot, mug or vase.

• If you're using dry flowers, leaves and twigs, arrange chunks of dry florist's foam on a smooth, flat surface, such as a rock, a piece of thick cardboard or a piece of driftwood.

**3** Poke your leaves, branches and flowers into the foam, arranging them into a wild 3-dimensional composition.

• Make it tall and willowy or short and stubby.

• Use a variety of shapes, sizes, textures and colors.

• Use some repetition in your composition.

• Make it symmetrical, or balanced. Or make it asymmetrical, or uneven.

**4** Use self-hardening clay and fun finds to add wild details you might see in your seasonal environment. A winter white rabbit? A spring robin? A cool crocodile? A beautiful butterfly?

**5** Display your composition on a tabletop or on a shelf in your room.

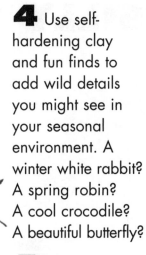

# Sketched Still Life

Use your display as inspiration for your next drawing or painting. It's the perfect still-life subject!

# SILLY SPROUTS

Turn a simple drawing idea into a sprouting sculpture.

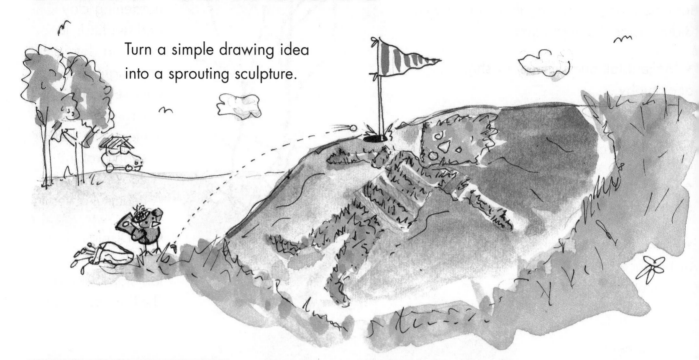

### Artist's Tools

- sketchbook and pencil
- patch of earth or empty flowerbox,* planting soil and rocks
- small shovel or trowel
- stick
- ruler
- grass seeds
- watering can and water
- sunshine
- rocks, pebbles, flowers, fun finds
- acrylic paint and paintbrushes

\* You can make a flower box by lining the inside of a cardboard box with a garbage bag.

**1** On a piece of paper, sketch out a silly but simple shape. Keep in mind the size of the space or flower box you're working in.

**2** Prepare your work area.

- Use a small shovel to prepare a sunny patch of garden by clearing and digging up the topsoil. This will make it easier to plant your seeds.

• Or put some rocks in the bottom of your flower box for drainage. Add at least 15 cm (6 in.) of soil. Put a tray or plastic bag under your flower box and place it by a sunny window.

**3** Use a stick to draw the shape you sketched into your soil. Add a little more soil within the lines so that the shape looks like a small mound or hill. Gently pat the soil down so the shape is clear and easy to see.

**4** Dampen your soil with a little water. Sprinkle the surface of the shaped mound with grass seeds. Don't forget to sprinkle or press in grass seeds on the sides of the mound. Cover your seeds with a light layer of soil.

**5** Use a watering can to gently water your freshly planted seeds.

**6** Be patient. After a week or two, the shape of your silly seedling sculpture should start to appear.

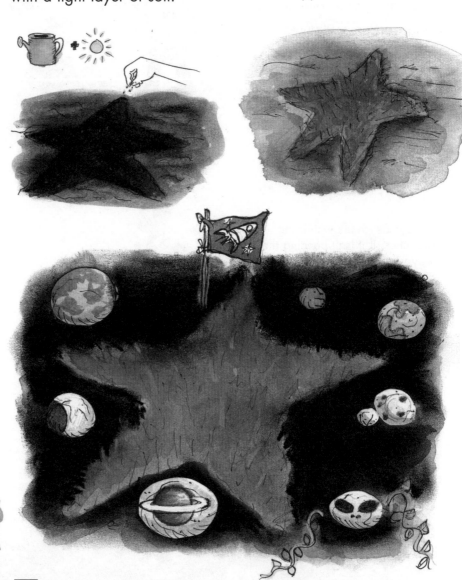

**7** Once the grass has grown in, embellish your living sculpture with painted rocks or pebbles, flowers or fun finds.

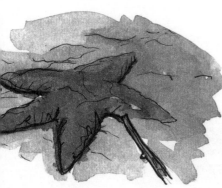

# TERRIFIC TOPIARIES

Artists and gardeners have been sculpting their green spaces for hundreds of years. Here are some suggestions for creating your own terrific living garden sculptures called topiaries.*

*Always be gentle with living branches. If it isn't bending the way you want, don't force it. Rethink or reshape your idea to keep the bush you're sculpting happy and healthy.

• Give climbing plants such as vines or ivy something to cling to. With an adult's help and wearing gloves and goggles, build a fun form out of chicken wire. Plant some vines that will grow and fill in your fun wire forms.

• Carefully cut and prune fast-growing, bushy herbs such as mint and rosemary with a pair of scissors. Keep your shapes simple but out of the ordinary.

• Gently bend and tie tender branches of bushes into unusual shapes and forms using string, florist's wire or pipe cleaners. Try bamboo poles or found sticks to hold your bushes' branches in place.

## Artist's Tip

Check out your local plant nursery and ask a gardening expert which bushes and vines grow well in the climate and conditions where you live.

# Flower Prints

Turn fresh leaves and flowers into prints that will never wilt.

**1** Cover your work area with a thick pile of newspapers or cardboard.

**2** Place a colorful flower or green leaf on a piece of paper or white cotton fabric.

**3** Place another piece of paper or fabric over top of the flower or leaf.

**4** Gently hammer your sandwiched flower with a mallet, hammer or smooth stone.

**5** Carefully pull apart your pieces of paper or fabric and remove the crushed leaves and flowers.

Check out these terrific prints — talk about flower power!

# Nature's Dyes and Stains

Some plants, vegetables and colorful flowers make excellent dyes and stains. Have an adult help you experiment — you might be surprised by the colors you create.

**1** Wash and very carefully cut colorful vegetables such as beets or spinach into small pieces. Or gather up some onion skins, grass or flowers.

**2** Carefully place your vegetables, plants or flowers into a large pot of boiling water.

**3** After everything boils for an hour or two, let your dye sit overnight and cool.

**4** Remove the vegetables or plants from the pot and pour your dye into a container through a strainer.

You can use your dye to paint paper. Or use it to dye fabulous fabrics.

# BEAUTIFUL BATIK

A batik is an Indonesian way of making art from wax, dye and cloth. The wax stops the dye from coloring the fabric, leaving behind a design or pattern. Try using an assortment of food coloring or vegetable dyes to create a beautiful batik.

## Artist's Tools

- sketchbook and pencil
- corrugated cardboard
- piece of untreated white cotton fabric
- white candle or crayons
- natural dyes (see page 53), food coloring or store-bought dyes*
- water
- paintbrushes
- permanent colored or metallic markers

\* Have an adult helper working with you if you are using store-bought dyes.

**1** In your sketchbook, practice drawing simple designs or patterns inspired by nature. Leaves, flowers, birds, fish and butterflies are all excellent subjects.

**2** Cover your work surface with lots of cardboard and spread your piece of cotton fabric over top.

**3** Use a candle or crayon to redraw your design on the fabric. Press very firmly so the wax sticks to the fabric.

**4** Brush some dye or food coloring over your piece of fabric. Adding water to your food coloring will make softer, lighter colors, while using pure food coloring makes bright, bold colors. Let dry.

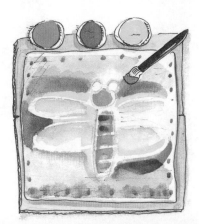

**5** Repeat step 4 using the same or, if you like, different colors of dye or food coloring. It's okay if your colors overlap or blend together.

**6** Add details and final touches with permanent or metallic markers.

## Artist's Tip

When using several colors of dye, it's a good idea to start with the lightest color (such as yellow) and end with the darkest (such as purple or dark blue).

# SOFT SNAKE SCULPTURE

You never know what artful ideas might be lurking in a pile of leftover leaves and grass ...

### Artist's Tools

- length of untreated canvas or roll of paper fabric
- newspaper and plastic sheet
- natural dyes (see page 53) or food coloring
- plastic containers and water
- paintbrushes
- oval or round leaves
- chalk pastels
- permanent or metallic markers
- dried grass clippings or newspapers
- glue gun or needle and thread
- seeds, beads or buttons

**1** Lay the canvas or paper fabric on a work surface that's been covered with a plastic sheet and lots of newspaper. The length of the fabric you use will be the length of your snake.

**2** Get your dyes ready or add food coloring to plastic containers filled with water. Brush the colors onto your paper fabric for the background of the snakeskin. (It's okay if your colors run or bleed together.) Let dry.

**3** Place a leaf on your painted snakeskin. Color the edges of the leaf with a chalk pastel. With your fingers, rub the pastel over the leaf's edges onto the snakeskin. Lift your leaf to reveal a scaly print. Repeat using different colors and overlapping the leaf until your snakeskin is covered with a colorful scalelike pattern.

**4** Use permanent or metallic markers to outline some of your leafy scales or to add other patterns and designs.

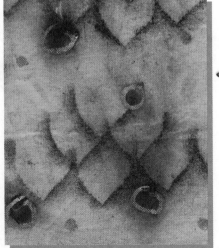

**5** Fold your snakeskin lengthwise. With an adult's help, sew or hot-glue the edges together, leaving the top and a bit of the side open.

**6** Stuff your snakeskin with dried grass clippings or balled-up newspapers.

**7** Sew or glue the opening closed.

**8** Attach a twig or ribbon tongue and buttons, seeds or beads for the eyes. S-s-s-super!

## A Sneaky Snake Installation

A temporary, outdoor snakelike sculpture can be as simple as a long line of overlapping leaves and flower petals held in place with smooth stones and topped with a pointy twig tongue.

# PERFECTLY PRESSED

A collection of found leaves and flowers is the perfect starting point for making interesting images and fun forms! No matter where you live or what the season, a quick walk outdoors (or a trip to a garden store) will produce some lovely, leafy finds.

## Artist's Tools

- collection of fresh leaves or flowers
- construction paper, old painting projects or untreated canvas
- wax paper
- heavy books
- scissors
- white glue
- colored pencils, metallic markers or acrylic paint

**1** Collect some freshly fallen leaves or cut flowers. Look for a variety of shapes, colors and textures. Your leaves will dry and crinkle up quickly, so don't wait too long to use them.

**2** Place your favorite finds between two sheets of wax paper and press them between two heavy, flat objects, such as books. Keep your finds pressed for a few days or even a week.

**3** Carefully remove your pressed finds from the wax paper.

**4** Arrange your collection of pressed leaves and flowers on a flat surface. What can you make? Animals? Insects? Silly scenes?

• Create contrasts by using leaves that are very different in size, shape, texture and color.

• Layer your leaves to make a variety of details and interesting images.

• Cut some leaves for some detailed final touches.

**5** Find a background best that shows off your fabulous foliage creation. Try

• brightly colored construction paper

• finished painting projects

• pieces of untreated canvas

**6** Piece by piece, brush a bit of white glue on the back of your pressed leaves and flowers and glue your organic collage onto the background. After the glue dries, draw or dab on colorful details.

# BIZARRE BOTANICALS

Botanicals are delicate watercolor paintings of plants. Have some fun and make your botanical bizarre looking!

## Artist's Tools

- plant sample
- pencil and eraser
- watercolor paints and water
- watercolor paintbrushes
- watercolor paper
- fine felt-tip markers
- old magazines, scissors and glue

**1** Set up a simple plant sample. Try to find a sample that still has its roots by collecting plants that have been weeded from a garden or by carefully removing a small plant from its pot and gently shaking off the excess soil around the root. (You can place a living plant in a glass of water while you're studying it so it can be replanted when you are done.)

**2** Use your pencil to sketch your plant very lightly on the watercolor paper.

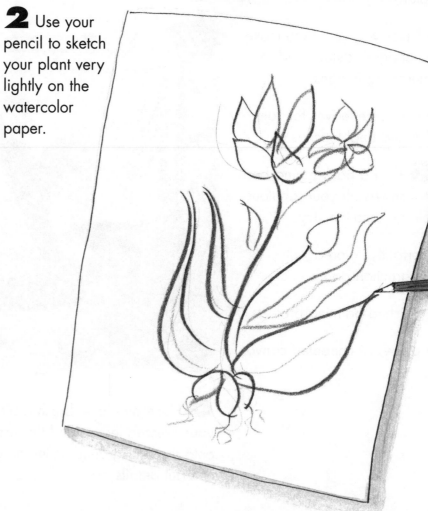

**3** Wet your brush with some water, and use a scrap of paper to experiment with mixing and blending the colors you see in your plant.

• The more water you add to your paint, the lighter it will be. Less water will make your colors stronger.

• Practice blending your colors from lightest to darkest.

**4** When you're ready, fill in your drawing with a coat of watery paint. Let dry.

**5** Look carefully at your plant sample. Brush on some less watery paint where the colors of your botanical should be darker. Let dry.

**6** Add shadows to the underside of the leaves, stems and flowers by brushing on watery blues, dark greens and purples. Let dry.

**7** Use white paint or drops of water to add delicate highlights, or light spots. Let dry.

**8** With a tiny brush or fine felt-tip markers, add finishing touches, like delicate roots, veins or flower centers. Let dry.

**9** Now turn your botanical into a bizarre beauty.

• Draw in tiny creatures you imagine might live on or underneath your beautiful blooms.

• Paint or collage strange leaves and flowers that might grow from your plant.

• Label your botanical with a weird and wacky name.

Coo-Coo Carnivorous Imagideellious

# WOVEN WONDERS

Weave long leaves, vines, stems, straw or grass into incredible sculptural shapes. Follow a few simple steps to learn how to weave your best ideas into wonderful works of art.

## Before You Begin

• Collect vines and tall grasses on a walk outdoors. Or, they can be bought at a garden center or plant nursery. Try asking a neighbor or gardener for leftover branches, twigs and stems from a cut tree or landscaping project.

• Soak vines or thin branches in water overnight to soften them for bending.

• Raffia is a long grass great for weaving and braiding. It's found in any craft shop.

## Tips

• Twisted, tied and braided grass, stems, vines or long flowering plants can be used for making wreaths or circular sculptures.

• Let the natural bends and curves of your weaving materials inspire the forms you make.

• You can create whimsical weavers and stakes that will add fun curls and curves to your work. Use string to tightly tie fresh, flexible vines and stalks around objects such as a ball, bottle or can and set them in the sun until they are completely dried out.

# Weaving

• Collect some long, flexible plant pieces. These are the "weavers." Tall grass, hay and raffia all make excellent weavers.

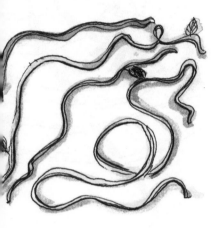

• Your smaller, stronger pieces of wood or vines are the "stakes."

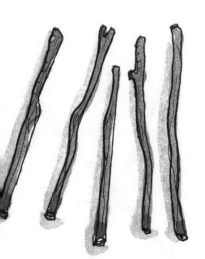

**1** On a smooth work surface, line your stakes up, one beside the other.

**2** One at a time, pass your weavers over and under your stakes.

**3** Repeat this step until you run out of weavers or room on your stakes.

**4** Fill in any gaps or holes with grass, leaves or dried flowers.

**5** Go a step further and combine a number of woven wonders to make a silly sculpture.

# SUPER SPIDER'S WEB

All it takes is some simple
weaving to spin your own
super spider's web.

- collection of small branches, twigs and vines
- florist's wire
- raffia

**1** Collect an assortment of
bendable vines, twigs and
small, thin branches.

**2** Make two Xs using your four longest branches or twigs.
Tie each X tightly together in the center with some florist's wire.
You may need to pull off some small branches or leaves if they
get in the way.

**3** Attach your two X shapes to one another with more florist's wire so they make a star. This is the frame of your web.

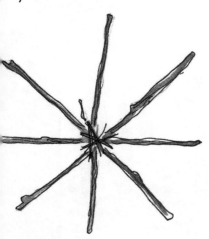

**4** Tie the end of a length of rafia close to the center of your star shape.

**5** Weave the raffia around the frame of the web to make a spiral pattern. As you go, wrap the raffia around each stick of the frame to hold it in place.

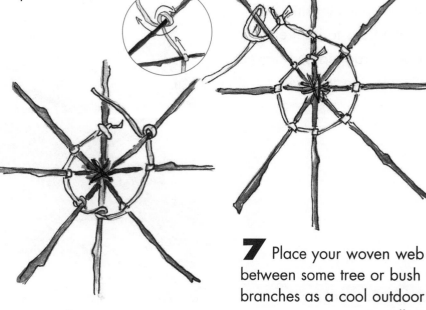

**6** When you are close to running out of raffia, tie the end to another long piece and continue weaving.

**7** Place your woven web between some tree or bush branches as a cool outdoor installation piece.

Bring the web to life by tying on an incredible creepy crawler (see page 68).

# AMAZING INSECTS AND ARACHNIDS

Explore a nearby garden or green space looking for beautiful bugs to inspire this dripped, dragged and blown watercolor masterpiece.

## Artist's Tools

- watercolor paints
- watercolor paintbrushes and water
- bristol board
- pin or small stick
- piece of string or thread
- drinking straw
- felt-tip pens, markers or colored pencils
- metallic markers
- acrylic paint
- glitter or shiny nail polish

**1** Wet a watercolor brush with lots of water and dip it into some paint. Squeeze your paint-filled brush between your thumb and finger until a few drops of watery paint plop onto your page. How many body parts does your insect or arachnid have? Two? Three? Ten?

**2** Add long legs and amazing antennae to your insect's paint-drop body.

• Blow through a straw to blast big fat paint drops into an explosion of long legs.

• Dip a piece of string or thread into your paint and pull it into silly scribbles.

• Use a pin or stick to drag your paint drops in different directions.

**3** Let your watercolor drawings dry completely.

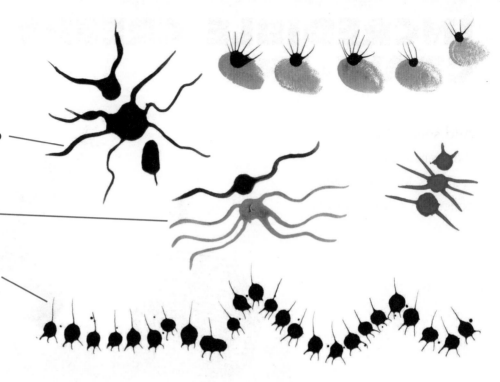

**4** Draw in some details on your beautiful bugs.

• Sketch smaller details with fine felt-tip pens, markers or colored pencils.

• Use metallic markers to add shiny details.

• Dab on glitter, nail polish or acrylic paint to add finishing touches to gorgeous insect wings.

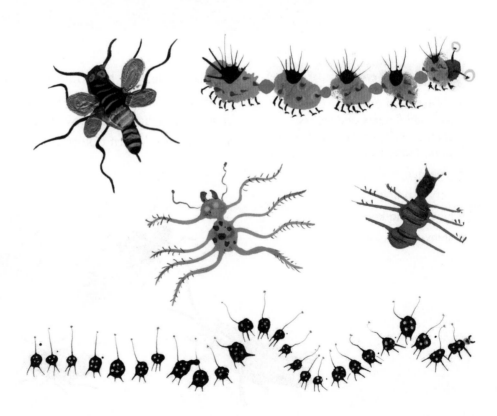

# INCREDIBLE CREEPY CRAWLERS

Add some of these 3-dimensional creepy crawlers to your growing collection of outdoor art.

## Artist's Tools

- collection of organic materials (pressed flowers and leaves, seeds, shells, grass, wood, sticks, bark, moss, etc.)
- glue gun and gloves
- acrylic paints
- metallic markers
- shiny nail polish

**1** Look outside for some insect inspiration. Or check out some books, magazines or the Internet for information on insects or arachnids. How many legs, body parts or wings do you see? What colors do you need?

**2** Arrange your collection of leaves, seeds, shells, grass, wood, sticks and vines into some insect formations.

• Seeds, shells, and worn and weathered pieces of wood make great body parts.

• Skinny sticks, roots and vines can be bent and shaped into terrific legs or antennae.

• Pressed flower petals or leaves make wonderful wings (see page 58).

• Bark, moss or woven grass can add wonderful textures and colors.

**3** With an adult's help, carefully attach your insect's body parts using a bit of glue.

**4** Add touches of color to your insects and arachnids with

• acrylic paints or stains

• metallic markers

• shiny nail polish

Your creepy crawly creations will look wonderful arranged on a shelf, tabletop or balcony, in a backyard ...

Or see page 64 to weave a web to display your incredible creepy crawlers.

# Barking up a Tree

The bark of an old, dead tree branch or stump can be pulled off with your hands or cut off with scissors.

• Papery thin strips of bark can be drawn on or cut with scissors into neat patterns, shapes and forms to add interesting elements to your art.

• Smooth pieces of bark can be stained with watery acrylic paints or vegetable dyes or smudged with colorful chalk pastels.

• A interestingly shaped piece of bark can be the starting point for a cool sketchbook study.

# Completely Stumped

Fallen or broken branches and tree stumps are a fantastic find. Check around your neighborhood after a big storm or wildly windy night and ask your neighbors if you can have any fallen wood.

Wood from a dead, dried tree or branch can be

• stripped of its bark

• sanded smooth with sandpaper

• stained with watered-down acrylic paints or vegetable dyes

• stacked into cool sculptural forms

## Artist's Tip

Let the knots, grooves and natural grain of your wood inspire the shapes and forms for your cool constructions. Wood grain is the direction that the lines or fibers in the wood grow in.

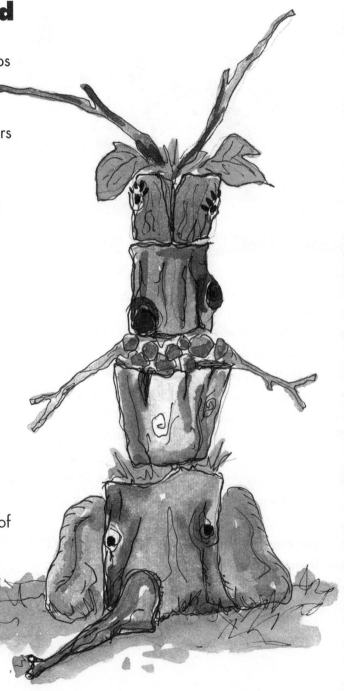

# LIVING LAWN SCULPTURE

A lawn sculpture is a fun way to display your great, green art!

## Artist's Tools

- spade or shovel
- collection of bamboo poles, garden sticks or long branches
- painted fabric (see page 56)
- large cardboard box
- acrylic paints and paintbrushes
- plants or topiaries (see page 50)
- collection of rocks, stones, tree stumps and bark

**1** On a sunny day, find a grassy piece of lawn you have permission to work on. (You can create a smaller-scale living sculpture with twigs in a flowerpot filled with soil.)

**2** Think of a simple design to fill your space. Use a spade or small shovel to make some narrow slits in the grass or soil in this shape.

**3** Poke your collection of branches, bamboo poles or garden sticks firmly into the slits. Stomp on the grass or press down the soil at the base of each one. Try planting your stick or poles

- straight up and down

- at an angle

- at different depths

- different distances apart

**4** Weave some colorful fabric in and out of the planted sticks.

**5** Paint a large cardboard box and turn your lawn sculpture into a perfect playground.

**6** Plant some flowers or place some topiaries around the base of your sculpture to add color and fun forms.

**7** Rocks, stones, stumps and bark are all great materials you can use to add solidly delightful details to your living lawn sculpture.

# It's All Elemental

An outdoor art adventurer finds inspiration in wind, water and sunshine for artful ideas that soar, flow and grow!

**Great Flowing Fountain**
(page 90)

**Things with Wings**
(page 81)

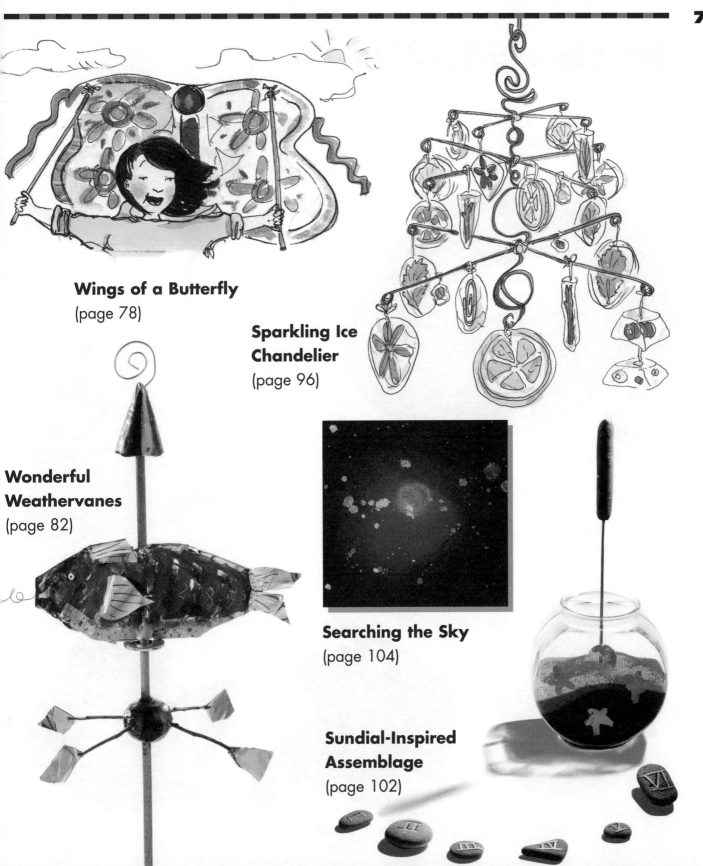

**Wings of a Butterfly**
(page 78)

**Sparkling Ice Chandelier**
(page 96)

**Wonderful Weathervanes**
(page 82)

**Searching the Sky**
(page 104)

**Sundial-Inspired Assemblage**
(page 102)

# In the Studio

These are some tools and materials to help you explore the elements.

feathers

hose

sprinkler

chalk pastels

tissue paper

fishing wire

watering can

magnifying glass

string

construction paper

# WINGS OF A BUTTERFLY

Turn a symmetrical printing project into a pair of wings that catches the wind and sends your spirits soaring.

## Artist's Tools

- large sheet of clear, strong plastic
- newspapers
- permanent marker
- scissors
- plastic containers
- acrylic paint and paintbrushes
- liquid dish soap
- colored tissue paper or cellophane
- 2 sturdy sticks or wooden dowels about 30 cm (12 in.) long
- duct tape
- strong string
- streamers or feathers

**1** Think about the butterflies you have seen, or look at pictures in books, magazines or on the Internet. Notice the shapes, colors and patterns of butterflies' wings.

**2** Fold your sheet of clear plastic in half and lay it flat on a work surface covered with newspapers. Use a permanent marker to draw a large wing shape. The wing should begin and end on the fold and be about as wide as your arm.

**3** Carefully cut out your wing shape. Cut through both layers of plastic, but do not cut along the fold. Unfold your cut-out wings and lay them flat on your work surface.

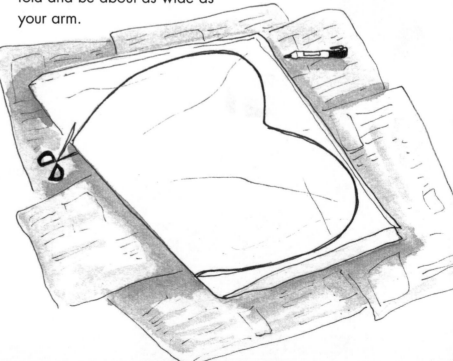

**4** In plastic containers, add a drop or two of dish soap to a few acrylic paints. On one half of your butterfly wings, plop a few fat drops of paint and brush on some bold patterns.

**5** While the paint is wet, fold the other half of your plastic wings over. Gently smooth the plastic with your hands. Carefully unfold your wings again (you may need a helping hand).

**6** Add some decorative details while the paint is wet.

• Use the handle tip of your brush to scratch in patterns.

• Press on colored tissue paper or cellophane cutouts.

• Brush on a few outlines or more colors.
Let dry.

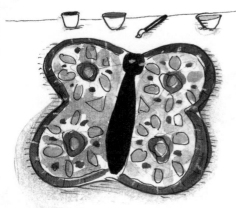

**7** Flip your wings over, painted side down. Attach a stick or dowel to each wing tip using a few pieces of tape. Secure the sticks by wrapping strong string around the taped part.

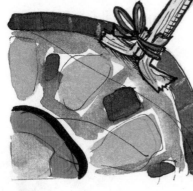

**8** Add some colorful streamers, tissue or feathers to your beautiful butterfly wings with tape or string.

On the next breezy day, take hold of your wings with a stick or dowel in each hand and go for a run.

# Light as a Feather

Start with a found feather as the inspiration for a chalk pastel sketch that looks light enough to float away.

**1** Sketch the shape of the feather.

**2** Lightly draw in some of the colors you see. If your feather is all one color, add white for soft highlights and brown, black or purple for shadows.

**3** Create a feathery-soft texture by rubbing and blending in a few of the colors with your finger.

**4** Add delicate details, spots or speckles.

# Things with Wings

Make your own flying creatures using pictures cut out of old magazines.

**1** Mix and match the cutouts until you're happy with your crazy creatures.

**2** Glue your cutouts to stiff paper or cardboard. If you need to, draw in wings using chalk pastels or colored pencils.

**3** Cut your winged things out.

• Glue your fun flying things to an interesting background, such as an old drawing or painting.

• Glue your fun flying things to some clear plastic wrap with white glue and tape them to your window.

# WONDERFUL WEATHERVANES

A weathervane is an artful instrument used to show which direction the wind is blowing. This sculpture twists and turns when the wind blows!

## Artist's Tools

- large piece of bristol board or copper foil*
- gloves and safety goggles
- pencil
- scissors
- white glue
- aluminum foil
- aluminum pie plate
- acrylic paints and paintbrushes or permanent markers
- wooden dowel, at least 30 cm (12 in.) long
- glue gun and gloves or duct tape
- metal washer (big enough to fit the wooden dowel through)
- vegetable oil
- self-hardening clay
- 4 small sticks or wooden skewers
- fun finds (streamers, sticks, feathers, etc.)

* Copper foil is found in art supply stores. Wear gloves and safety goggles when cutting it.

## Create an Ornament

The ornament is the part of a weathervane that moves and turns with the wind.

**1** Fold your bristol board or copper foil in half. Starting and ending on the fold, draw a simple shape. It should be longer than it is deep. It should also have different-looking ends, like an arrow, or a head and a tail, like a dragon or a fish. This will help you tell which direction you ornament is facing.

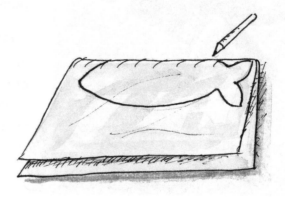

**2** Cut your shape out without cutting along the fold.

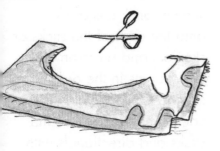

**3** Unfold the board or foil. If you're using bristol board, weatherproof the ornament by brushing some white glue over the entire shape and covering it completely with aluminum foil.

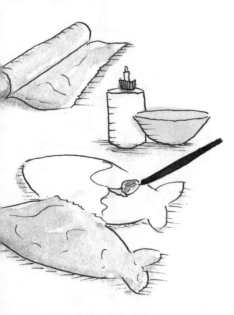

## Make the Directionals

North? South? East? West? The directionals are the part of a weathervane that point to the four directions as the ornament blows around.

**4** Cut out four small, simple shapes from copper foil or from an aluminum pie plate.

**5** Use permanent markers or acrylic paints to write a letter for each of the directions (N, S, E and W) on the shapes.

## Assemble Your Weathervane

**6** Refold your ornament loosely over one end of your wooden dowel. The dowel should be centered. Use duct tape or hot glue to close the edges of the ornament. Have an adult help if you are using a glue gun.

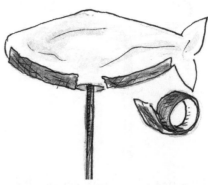

**7** Use scissors to carefully cut or poke a hole in the middle of the ornament, along the fold. Slide the end of the dowel up through the hole 13 to 15 cm (5 to 6 in.).

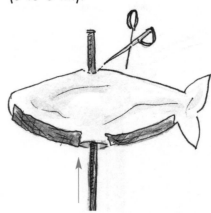

**8** Slide a metal washer up the dowel to the base of the ornament. Test to make sure your ornament is balanced on the top of the washer and that it spins easily when you blow on either end.

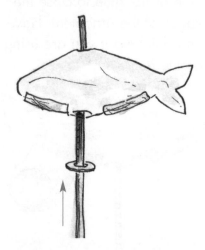

Use hot glue (with an adult's help) or duct tape to hold your washer in place, and add a drop of vegetable oil to the top of your washer so your ornament spins easily.

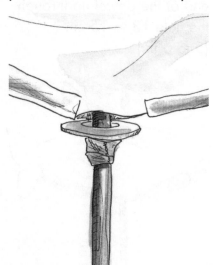

**9** Roll out a ball of self-hardening clay that's about the size of your fist. Poke the end of the wooden dowel through. Move the ball of clay up the dowel until it is at least 5 cm (2 in.) or so below the bottom of the washer.

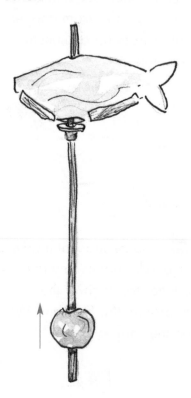

**10** Press the sticks or skewers into the clay ball. Space them equally, as shown. Stick bits of clay onto the ends of the sticks or skewers and press on the directionals in the order shown. Once the clay is completely dry, secure the sticks and directionals with hot glue or duct tape.

# Fun Final Touches

**11** Add some fun final touches, such as

• acrylic paint colors

• plastic streamers or feathers

• a finial, or decorative top, made from foil, clay or fun finds

**12** Plant your weathervane in the garden or lawn and watch the way the wind blows. You can use a compass to show you which way the directionals should point.

# Bubble Painting

Try this idea for a cool wind- and water-inspired painting experiment.

**1** Cover your work surface with lots of newspapers.

**2** Add a drop or two of dish soap to some plastic bowls filled with watery tempera paints.

**3** Put a straw into one bowl and blow. Keep blowing until there are lots of big, beautiful bubbles flowing over the top of the bowl.

**4** Gently place a piece of paper over the bubbles.

**5** Check out the cool marks left behind when you lift the paper off.

**6** Repeat steps 3 to 5 with different colors of paint. Let dry.

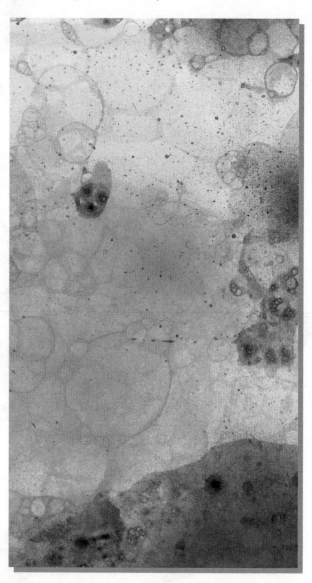

It's a bubbly background to paint or draw on.

# Marvelous Marbling

Here's how to create some watery patterns on paper if you don't have a store-bought marbling kit.

**1** Put a few drops of vegetable oil into a pie plate filled with water.

**2** Add a bit of water to some of your favorite colors of acrylic paint. Gently spoon a little of each color onto the surface of the oil and water mixture.

**3** Use a toothpick to gently stir a colorful pattern.

**4** Lay paper over your oil and paint mixtures so they just touch.

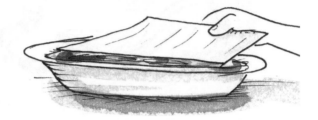

**5** Carefully lift the paper off. Let dry on some paper towel.

It's a watery background to paint or draw on.

# COOL CORAL REEF

Dive into this amazing underwater world.

## Artist's Tools

- newspapers
- large sheet of watercolor or craft paper
- masking tape
- spray bottle and water
- acrylic paints and large paintbrushes
- sea sponge or paper towels
- food coloring or acrylic inks
- sea salt
- chalk pastels
- old nature magazines
- scissors

**1** Tape the edges of a large piece of watercolor or craft paper to a newspaper-covered work surface.

**2** Use a spray bottle filled with water to wet your paper thoroughly.

**3** Brush on some ocean-inspired background colors of acrylic paint.

**4** While your page is still wet, dab a sponge or paper towel over parts of your page to "lift off" the paint and make watery patterns.

**5** If your page has dried, spray it again. Drip drops of bright acrylic inks or food coloring over your page, letting them bleed, stain, run and spread.

**6** Sprinkle some sea salt over your wet, watery page for coral-like patterns. Let dry.

**7** Add fishy final touches.

• Draw in cool coral reef creatures with chalk pastels.

• Make a collage of fish and coral cutouts from old magazines.

### Artist's Tip

Remember the rules of perspective when you're adding your final touches: the closer things are, the larger they look, and the farther away things are, the smaller they look.

# GREAT FLOWING FOUNTAIN

Open the floodgates to your imagination and build a wonderful water sculpture.

## Artist's Tools

- smooth stones or large, flat rocks
- collection of waterproof containers (old buckets, mixing bowls, large metal pans, plastic birdbaths, plastic cups, etc.)*
- acrylic paints and paintbrushes
- vegetable dyes
- fun finds (flowers, branches, shells, stones, etc.)
- glue
- food coloring
- aluminum pies plates
- hammer and nail
- copper refrigerator coil (an option found in hardware stores)
- self-hardening clay
- hose, sprinkler and water can

* Be sure you have permission to use these.

## Choose a Spot

• If you're working outdoors, make sure you set your fountain up in a place where it's okay for water to spill and flow, such as a grassy spot in your backyard.

• If you're working indoors, build your small fountain in a waterproof bin, tub or bucket. Remember that you'll need to empty the fountain, so make sure you're near a sink or tub drain.

# Build a Basic Fountain Structure

**1** Build a base for your fountain by stacking some smooth rocks or stones in interesting piles or sculptural shape. Test your base to be sure it is solid and sturdy.

**2** Balance a basin, or container that catches the water, on top of your rock base. Buckets, mixing bowls, metal baking pans or plastic birdbaths all make great fountain basins. Try stacking your containers to create a leveled look.

**3** Decorate the outside of the basin.

• Dab on some acrylic paint to add pure bright color.

• Glue shells, smooth pebbles or beads to your fountain's basin.

• Pile on river rocks and smooth stones or add some vines and branches.

• Use vegetable dye (see page 53) or acrylic paints mixed with water to stain stones or sanded branches.

## Top Off Your Fountain

**4** Have fun finishing your fountain.

• Assemble a pyramid of clear plastic cups or containers over the top. Add tiny drops of food coloring to each of your cups or containers for a rainbow waterfall effect.

• Make some art for the ears. With an adult's help, use a hammer and nail to poke a few holes into a collection of pie plates. Be sure to wear gloves and goggles.

• Attach fun final touches such as a coiled curlicue topped with a simple sculptural shape made of clay.

## Just Add Water

**5** Use a hose, sprinkler, watering can or tap to pour water over your fountain structure, or just wait for a rainy day.

Placing a water pump in the basin of your fountain will help keep your fountain flowing. You can buy an inexpensive water pump at many craft shops, plant nurseries or hardware stores.

# Freezing Points

Try some of these ice-sculpting techniques.

**1** Pour water into plastic or paper containers such as empty milk cartons or ice-cube trays. If you like, add food coloring, beads, small toys, slices of fruit. If you want your sculptures to stand tall, place a piece of aluminum foil over the tray or container and insert twigs, pencils or Popsicle sticks. Put the containers in a freezer overnight.

• Use Plasticine or modeling clay to make sturdy bases.

• Use a fork to scrape and carve drawings or details.

• Use a nail file to chisel out small chunks.

• Use a spoon to scrape out small, rounded holes.

**2** Wear gloves and goggles while sculpting your icy-cold creations. And cover your work area with lots of towels and rags if you're working inside.

• Use warm water to melt edges into smooth round surfaces and to stick smaller pieces of ice together. *Never* use a hair dryer to melt your ice.

# Frozen Patterned Paper

Check out this cool painting project!

**1** Use water and a paintbrush to thoroughly wet some watercolor paper.

**2** Dab or drop on some colorful dots of acrylic inks or dyes.

**3** Place your paper in a freezer, and watch the frost patterns stain your page permanently.

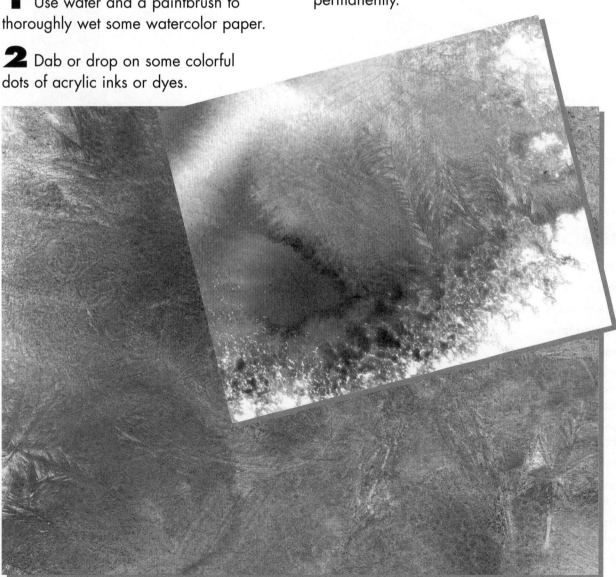

# SPARKLING ICE CHANDELIER

This sparkling temporary ice installation is great to try on a cold winter's day.

## Artist's Tools

- 3m (10 ft.) of 12-gauge wire
- tape measure
- wire cutters or pliers
- masking tape
- water
- collection of plastic containers (ice-cube trays, yogurt containers, etc.)
- fun finds (dried flowers, seeds, shells, slices of fruit, etc,)
- string or fishing wire
- freezer or below freezing weather
- plastic or glass beads and shiny gems
- gloves and safety goggles

## Make a Structure

**1** Wearing gloves and goggles and with help from an adult, cut a 120 cm (48 in.) piece of wire. Put it aside for later. Cut the rest of the wire into two pieces 15 cm (6 in.) long, two pieces 25 cm (10 in.) long and two pieces 30 cm (12 in.) long.

**2** Make an X with the two 15 cm (6 in.) pieces. Wrap the center of the X with masking tape to hold it in place. Make Xs out of the other two pairs of wire.

**3** Curl the ends of the Xs with the pliers to form little loops.

**4** Wrap one end of the 120 cm (48 in.) wire around the center of the biggest X. Bend some fun curls and loops into the wire, as shown.

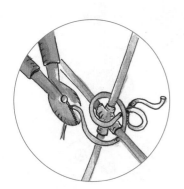

**5** A little farther up, wrap the wire around next biggest X. Bend some more curls, twist and loops into the wire.

**6** Repeat step 5 using the last X. If you run out of wire, cut and twist on another length of wire. Continue curling and looping the wire until you have a fancy chandelier frame you love.

## Make Sparkling Crystals

**7** Pour a little water into each of your plastic containers and drop in a few of your fun finds.

**8** Cut different lengths of string or fishing line and insert one end into each container. Freeze overnight.

**9** When the water is completely frozen, pop your frozen ice pieces out of their containers.

### Artist's Tip

Add a drop or two of food coloring at step 7 to make your crystals colorful.

## Assemble the Chandelier

**10** Working quickly (you might want a helper), tie your ice crystals to the curls and looped ends of the chandelier structure. Try to balance out your crystals so your chandelier hangs evenly.

**11** Tie on some sparkling beads or found crystal objects with fishing line or string for a shimmering finishing touch.

**12** Hang your finished sparkling chandelier outside and watch it sparkle in the sunlight.

Use a camera to document your ice sculpture before it melts.

# Silly Silhouettes

When you draw an outline of someone or something, you are drawing a silhouette. A sunny day, a sidewalk and sidewalk chalk are all you need to draw your friend's silly silhouette.

**1** Find a sidewalk where you have lots of room to draw. Have your friend strike a funny pose that casts a clear shadow.

**2** As you trace around the shadow, make sure you carefully draw all the details of your friend's silhouette.

**3** Try making your shadowy drawings at different times of the day. What differences do you see in shadows cast early in the morning, at noon or late in the day?

**4** Use charcoal or a pencil to copy your sidewalk shadow drawings into your sketchbook for funny, exaggerated figure studies.

# SOLAR-POWERED PRINTS

Try using the sun's light to create some beautiful photolike prints.

## Artist's Tools

- sunny day
- several sheets of colorful construction paper
- collection of flat objects with distinct shapes (large leaf, glove, starfish, key, etc.)
- chalk pastels

**1** On a sunny day, spread a few sheets of construction paper on a dry, flat sunny spot outside or under a bright window.

**2** Arrange your collection of interesting objects on top of the construction paper. If you're working outside, you may need to weigh down your objects or the corners of your construction with small stones.

**3** After two or three hours, carefully lift one of your objects up to see if the construction paper surrounding your object has faded.

## Other Sun-Print Creations

• Put one or more of your objects back in the same spot on your page and leave it in the sun for a few more hours for an even stronger outline.

• Try moving or turning your objects slightly. After another hour or two, you'll see a layered, shadowy effect starting to emerge.

• Make a series of sun prints with a theme, such as a collection of different leaf shapes.

• Arrange your objects to form a scene or story.

• Use chalk pastels to draw delicate details on your prints.

## On Camera

A camera works in a similar way as your sun prints, only much faster. Every time you take a "snapshot," your camera lets light shine through its lens. The light leaves a mark or impression on special light-sensitive film inside.

# SUNDIAL-INSPIRED ASSEMBLAGE

On a sunny day, watch time fly by making an assemblage — a collection of 3-dimensional forms — designed to cast cool shadows.

**1** Assemble a fun 3-dimensional form that has a tall centerpiece that will cast a long shadow. Try

- a long, skinny branch with a glove tied to its end

- a plastic birdbath with a basketball sitting in its center

- a wooden spoon wrapped in wire curlicues

- a silly-looking flyswatter

**2** Plant your object in a sunny spot that's completely clear of clutter. The middle of an empty sandbox, a green lawn or a flowerpot are great places for your 3-dimensional form.

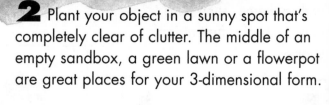

**3** At the beginning of each hour, mark the spot where your object's shadow falls with a special stone, shell, pebble or bead. Try to mark every hour from sunup to sundown. You can write, draw or paint the hour on the marker if you like.

Check out the crazy clock you just created. It's a solar-powered assemblage that will help you keep track of time!

## Amazing Instrument

A sundial is an instrument for telling time. As the sun moves across the sky, the shadow cast by the dial moves, too. Each season, the shadows fall in the same place at the same time each day. Where the shadow is tells people what time it is.

# SEARCHING THE SKY

Look up, up and away to search the sky for a picture-perfect view. Create a series of sky studies by looking at the changing sky at different times of day, during different weather conditions or during different seasons.

## Sky Series #1: A Sunny Blue Sky

### Artist's Tools

- acrylic paints and brushes
- sea sponge (optional)
- primed canvas or canvas board
- paint palette or aluminum pie plate

**1** Brush your canvas with a mixture of sky blue acrylic paint.

**2** While your canvas is still wet, blend in some white for soft fluffy clouds with a brush or a sea sponge.

**3** On your palette, mix in a tiny dab of yellow and white into some blue paint and brush in touches of turquoise.

**4** On your palette, mix together a tiny dab of red, blue and white to add some soft lavender shadows in your fluffy clouds.

# Sky Series #2: A Spectacular Sunset

## Artist's Tools

- watercolor paints and brushes
- water
- watercolor paper
- colored pencils and chalk pastels

**1** Dip your brush in water and wet your paper completely.

**2** Dip your brush in yellow paint and quickly brush it across the bottom of your wet paper.

**3** Dip your brush in orange paint and quickly brush it across the middle of your paper. Be sure to let it mix, stain and blend with the yellow.

**4** Dip your brush in red paint and quickly brush it across the top of your wet page, letting it mix and blend with a bit of the orange. Let dry.

**5** Use some colored pencils or chalk pastels to draw a setting sun, some soft pink and white clouds or a few birds flying by.

# Sky series #3: A Stormy Sky

## Artist's Tools

- newspapers
- white sketchbook or drawing paper
- graphite stick or soft pencil
- charcoal
- white acrylic paint
- very fine paintbrush

**1** Place your sketchbook or paper on a newspaper-covered work surface.

**2** Using heavy strokes going in one direction, scribble with the graphite or pencil over your entire page. The stronger and heavier your strokes, the stormier your sky will seem.

**3** For the horizon (where the sky and ground meet), rub some charcoal on your index finger and smudge it across the bottom of the page. (A low horizon will make your stormy sky seem extra eerie.)

**4** Add silhouettes of buildings and trees to your horizon.

**5** Add jagged streaks of lightning across your stormy sky with the white paint.

# Sky Series #4: A Cool Night Sky

## Artist's Tools

- newspapers
- chalk pastels
- dark blue or black construction paper
- tissues
- eraser
- white, yellow or silver acrylic paint
- old toothbrush

**1** On a newspaper-covered work surface, rub and blend heavy scribbles of dark blue and purple chalk pastels onto the paper using your finger or a tissue.

**2** Carefully erase some spots of the blended pastels until the paper shows through. Add a few tiny dots of white or yellow pastel, and gently blend them into your dark background with your fingertip for some big bright stars and planets.

**3** Dip the toothbrush into some white, yellow or silver acrylic paint and flick the toothbrush over your pastel-covered paper. Fill your page with lots of tiny, shimmering starry spots and speckles.

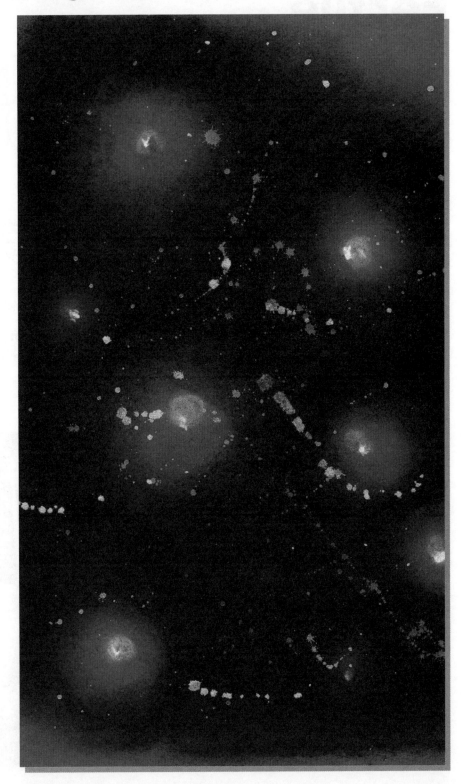

# Fertile Ground

In nature, nothing ever goes to waste. When something organic decays, or breaks down, it feeds the earth and helps new life grow. Find a whole crop of ideas in nature's cycles by using materials that are ready to be recycled or composted.

**Taking Root**
(page 112)

**Paper Re-productions**
(page 129)

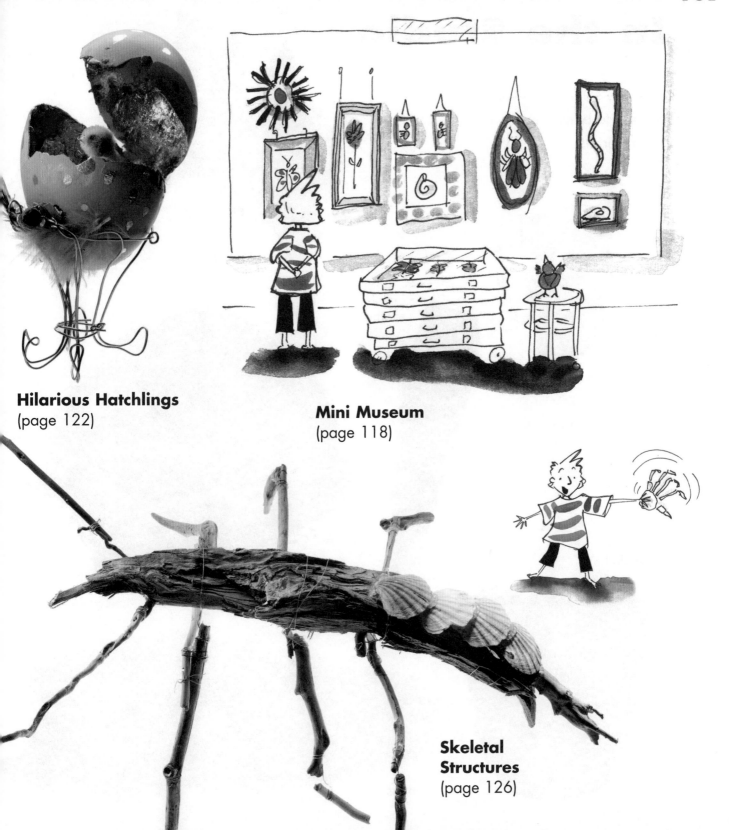

**Hilarious Hatchlings**
(page 122)

**Mini Museum**
(page 118)

**Skeletal
Structures**
(page 126)

# In the Studio

Here are some things you
can use to bring new life to
old materials.

leaves

feathers

blender

bucket

empty bird's nest

moss

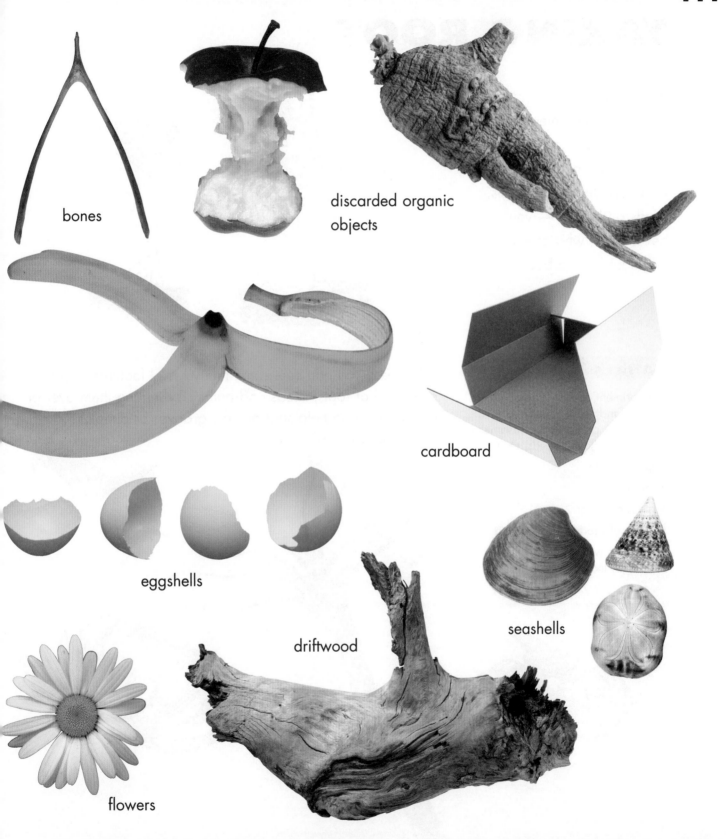

bones

discarded organic objects

cardboard

eggshells

seashells

driftwood

flowers

# TAKING ROOT

Root vegetables and bulbs come in lots of interesting shapes, sizes, colors and fun forms. Look up close at a collection of old roots, seeds and bulbs — you never know who or what might be staring back!

## Artist's Tools

- assortment of root vegetables, bulbs and seeds (beets, carrots, potatoes, garlic, leeks, sesame seeds, sunflower seeds, etc.)
- plastic knife
- toothpicks
- glass of water
- piece of fabric or paper bag
- fun finds (wire, beads, grass, flowers, leaves, shells, etc.)

**1** See if you can spot some funny facial features in your collection of roots, seeds and bulbs. Try turning them over or upside down to help spot bumps, grooves or dimples that remind you of funny faces.

**2** When you see the start a frown, long nose, winking eye or pointy ear, add the rest of your organic friend's features.

• If you like, place part of your root head in a glass of water in a sunny spot. After a few days, you may see hair or a beard starting to sprout!

• Use a plastic knife to make small starter cuts and press in some seeds and shells for eyes, ears and nostrils.

• Poke in a toothpick and attach another root or piece of a root for an extra-long chin or nose.

• Make a body for your funny root head with a piece of fabric or a paper bag and some fun finds.

# Staging a Scene

Make your root figure the star of a series of fun photographs. Set the stage for a simple funny scene using construction paper and other toys. Take a photo of each scene you create. Put your developed photos together so that they tell a simple story.

# REALLY ROTTEN FLIPBOOK

There's still a lot of life in an old apple core, banana peel or wilting flower. Here's how to turn an organic object you're ready to get rid of into a delightful "de-composition."

## Artist's Tools

- colored pencils and drawing paper or camera (and film, if needed)
- discarded organic object (banana peel, apple core, flower, etc.)
- construction paper
- scissors
- pencil and ruler
- glue gun and gloves

## Document the Decomposition

**1** Set your object in an open container where it won't be disturbed — or disturb others!

**2** Sketch or photograph your object every day for about 14 days in a row. (The warmer the temperature, the faster your object will decompose.) Make your images close-ups so that you can see the deteriorating details clearly. And sit in the same place each time you draw or photograph.

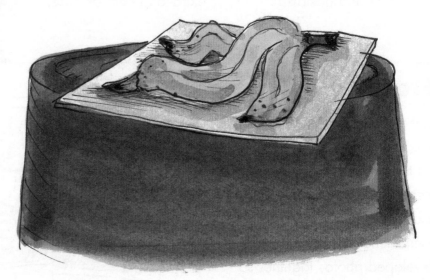

**3** Make sure you capture your object's

• changing colors

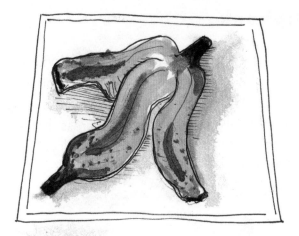

• changing shape

• changing texture

**4** If you're photographing your object, have your photos printed or developed.

Turn the page and find out how to bind your pages into a book form you can flip through.

## Make Your Flipbook

**5** Put your images in a pile in the same order they were drawn or photographed.

**6** Measure two times the width plus the depth of the pile. Then measure the length. Cut the construction paper into a rectangle this size.

**8** With an adult's help, fill the inside of the spine of your book with glue. Making sure your drawings or photos are stacked evenly, press the left edge of the stack into the glue. Let dry.

**7** Fold the paper around your pile of photos. Open the paper and mark the folds on either side of your pile of drawings or photos with a pencil. This is your book's spine.

## Artist's Tip

See page 129 to make paper out of pulp, and create cool paper to glue your sketched or photographed de-composition on.

**9** Decorate the outside of your flipbook with a drawing or a photocopy of your favorite photo.

Hold the spine of your book with your left hand and use your right hand to quickly flip the pages. Your object will decompose right before your eyes!

# Breaking Down

The process of decomposition is extremely important in nature. When natural objects or creatures die, their remains begin to break down and are absorbed into the earth, creating rich, fertile ground for new life to begin.

# MINI MUSEUM

A shadow box is a deep frame made for holding 3-dimensional art or objects. Create a mini museum by displaying cool collectibles and remarkable remains in a series of shadow boxes and fun frames.

## Artist's Tools

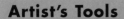

- collection of cool collectibles (dried flowers, feathers, shells, moss, etc.)
- Popsicle sticks
- white glue
- scissors
- balsa wood
- self-hardening clay
- cardboard, foam or cork tile
- jar lid and sticks or twigs
- aluminum or paper plate
- old muffin tin
- black acrylic paint and paintbrush or black construction paper
- double-sided tape or glue gun and gloves
- string and tape
- pushpins
- piece of plywood (optional)

**1** Start a collection of cool collectibles and really remarkable remains the next time you go for a walk outdoors. Keep an eye out for things others might overlook: dried flowers, an abandoned wasp or bees' nest, moss, broken eggshells, dropped feathers, seashells, sand dollars, etc.

**2** Make frames for your shadow boxes. Before you begin, think about what size and shape will best display your found objects.

• Build a deep-sided, square frame out of Popsicle sticks glued together with white glue.

• Make a box frame using balsa wood. Glue four pieces of wood onto a square or rectangle back using white glue around the edges.

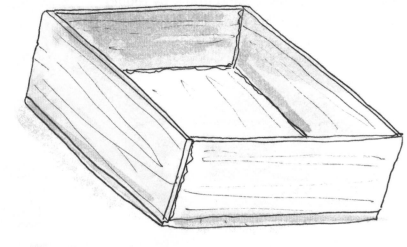

• Make a simple frame by gluing balls of hardened clay around the edges of a square of foam, cork tile or heavy cardboard.

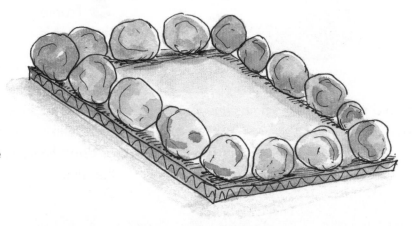

• Make a striking stick frame by gluing cut or broken twigs around the edge of a deep-sided jar lid. Work on a small section at a time.

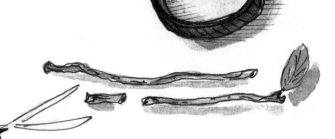

• Make an organic-looking frame by gluing dried moss or another grassy find around the edge of an aluminum or paper plate.

• Use an old muffin tin for frames for your tinier treasures.

**3** Once your shadow boxes and frames have dried, paint the insides black or glue on a piece of black construction paper. This will help your museum pieces stand out.

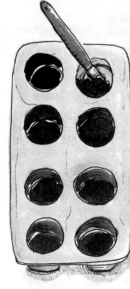

**4** Tape small pieces of string to the back of your shadow boxes for mounting your display later.

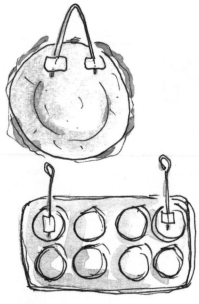

**5** Frame your cool collectibles and remarkable remains.

• Use small drops of glue or pushpins to gently attach delicate objects like feathers or dried flowers. Let the glue dry.

• Use double-sided tape or a glue gun (with an adult's help) to attach heavier objects like shells or stones. Let the glue dry.

**6** Arrange your boxes until you're happy with the look. Have a friend or adult help you carefully tack or nail them to the wall or a piece of plywood that you can lean against a wall for your cool miniature museum.

## Making a Scene

Make a mini scene, or diorama, inside a shadow box using several of your cool collectibles and some fun finds.

# HILARIOUS HATCHLINGS

Empty eggshells are the inspiration for these egg-cellent sculptures.

## Artist's Tools

- clean, empty eggshell*
- permanent markers
- food coloring or acrylic paints
- small paintbrush or toothbrush
- fun finds (seeds, flower petals, feathers, twigs, gold or silver foil, etc.)
- white glue and toothpick
- fine wire

* Remember, eggshells can be brittle and break easily, so be very careful while you work.

**1** Decorate your delicate shell by drawing patterns, designs or spots onto it with markers. Or brush or flick food coloring or acrylic paints over the surface of your shell with a paintbrush or toothbrush.

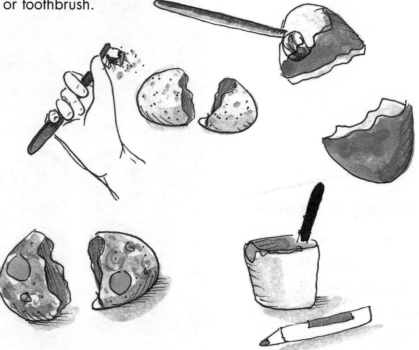

**2** Decorate your shell with delicate details made with fun finds.

• Extra bits of gold or silver foil or sparkles can be added to parts of your shell carefully brushed with white glue.

• Tiny creatures made from seeds, beads, leaves or flower buds can be added to the inside of your shell.

• Small feathers can be arranged or glued to your shell for a soft fluffy finish.

• Twist and bend fine wire into a delicate stand for your shell creation.

Try turning leftover fun finds into a creature you imagine hatching from your artfully decorated shell.

A cracked stick was inspiration for this fierce crocodile made with pinched pieces of clay and decorated with spots of acrylic paint.

# SWEPT AWAY

The tides will never leave you stranded when it comes to materials for sea-inspired sculptures. Get swept away by your imagination and give new life to some materials that have been washed ashore by the waves.

- smooth, dry piece of driftwood
- paintbrushes
- white glue
- sand
- chalk pastels
- acrylic paint, tempera paint or food coloring
- fun finds (seashells, seaweed, raffia, etc.)
- glue gun and gloves
- string or wire

**1** For your inspiration, think about your last trip to the beach, flip through some books on seas and oceans or look on the Internet. What would you find above and below the water?

**2** Begin with the background for your sculptural seascape.

• Brush white glue over parts of your driftwood and sprinkle on some sand for texture.

• Add chalk pastel lines or smudges and touches of acrylic or tempera paints for colorful details.

• A wash, or thin coat, of watered-down paint or food coloring can give your driftwood a nice underwater feel.

**3** Add your sea creatures to build the rest of your scene.

• Glue on some of your favorite finds.

• Glue clean, empty shells or pebbles together to make cool creatures such as sea snails and fun fish.

• Use string or wire to tie dried bits of raffia or seaweed pieces to water-worn sticks or smooth stones and make silly squids and sea creatures.

# Underwater World

See page 88 for making watermarks and create a painted background that looks like an underwater world for your sea sculpture to be mounted on.

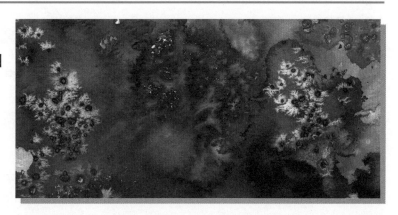

# SKELETAL STRUCTURES

Get to the bare bones of the matter and transform an assortment of old branches and twigs into a skeletal structure of a creature past or present.

## Artist's Tools

- collection of dried branches, twigs or pieces of driftwood
- newspapers
- sandpaper
- plastic container and water
- white acrylic paint and paintbrush
- picture-hanging wire
- pliers or wire cutters
- gloves and safety goggles
- glue gun

**1** Spread out your collection of dried, broken branches, twigs, sticks or pieces of driftwood on a flat surface covered with newspapers.

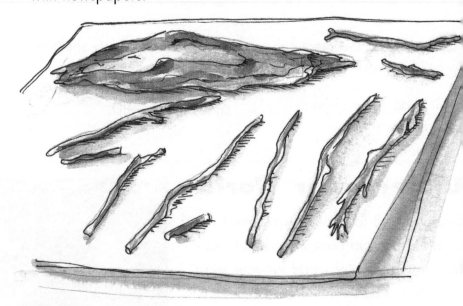

**2** If there is bark on the branches, peel off as much as you can. Sand all your sticks and branches smooth with sandpaper.

**3** In a plastic container, mix water into some white acrylic paint until you have a watery, milky mixture. Paint your sanded sticks, branches and twigs and let dry. Letting your wood dry in the hot sun might create neat cracks for a great aged effect.

**4** Wearing gloves and goggles, twist a piece of wire tightly around one end of each of your dried wooden bones. Using pliers will help. Make sure you leave an extra 8 to 10 cm (3 to 4 in.) of wire at the end of the twist.

**5** Lay out all of your wooden bones back on the flat surface. Move them around and experiment with making different skeletal shapes. What kind of structure will you form with your cool wooden bone collection? A tiny ocean organism? A winged prehistoric creature? A human hand?

**6** When you've created your skeletal structure, twist the wired ends of your bones together. With an adult's help, use your pliers or wire cutters to trim off any excess wire. Use a drop of glue to hold loose wire in place.

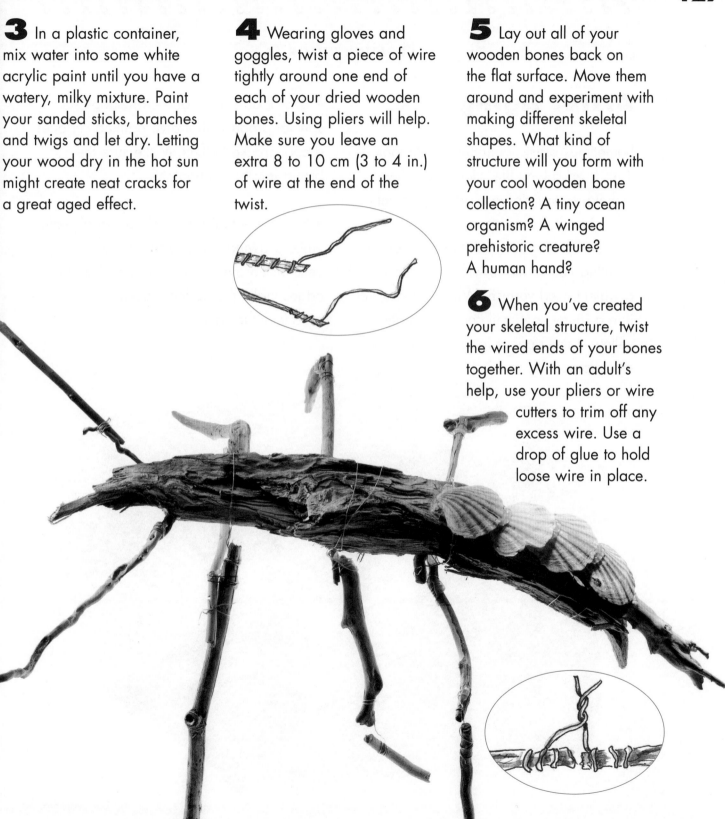

# Artful Aging

Sometimes artists want their art to look as if it's lived a long life. Here are a few techniques to help your art look ancient.

• In an open space, paint over an acrylic painting you've made with several coats of a water-based varnish. When it is dry, set it in a sunny spot until cool cracks and yellow stains appear for a marvelous old masterpiece.

• Lots of art supply and craft shops sell special products that give painted surfaces a cool cracked effect. Make sure the brand you buy is nontoxic.

• Rub a wet teabag over a scrap of plain white drawing paper and let dry. The yellowish-brown stain and ripped and torn edges make the perfect background for an ancient treasure map.

# PAPER RE-PRODUCTIONS

Don't throw old paper projects and silly scraps away! Recycle them into awesome paper "re-productions."

## Artist's Tools

- scrap paper
- water
- measuring cup and spoons
- blender
- wallpaper paste
- small bits of leaves, grass or flowers
- newspapers
- paper towels or cheesecloth
- iron and clean, old rags

**1** Tear scrap paper into small pieces and fill an unplugged blender. Add 250 mL (1 cup) of water. Let the paper soak until completely soft.

**2** Add 25 to 40 mL (2 to 3 tbsp) of wallpaper paste to the soggy mixture. With an adult's help, plug in the blender, put the lid on and blend the mixture.

• Try blending in different types of grass or flower petals to turn your pulp different colors.

• For an organic look, mix bits of leaves, grass or tiny flowers into your pulp mixture after you remove it from the blender.

**3** Cover a flat work surface in a thick layer of newspaper and spread out the paper towels or cheesecloth.

**4** Unplug the blender and scoop out a cupful of blended pulp. Spread it out over the paper towels or cheesecloth.

• Spread an even 0.5 cm (1/4 in.) thick layer of pulp mixture for great drawing and printing paper.

• Spread a very thin layer of pulp mixture for delicate, lacy paper.

• Spread a thick layer of pulp mixture for chunky paper that can be pinched and squeezed into 3-dimensional forms as it dries.

**5** After it's spread out on the cheesecloth or paper towels, shape the pulp. Your paper can be any shape you want: square, oval, star …

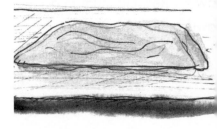

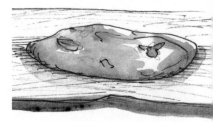

**6** Carefully place your paper (including the paper towels or cheesecloth) on a warm, flat spot to dry.

**7** Carefully peel your sheet of paper off your paper towels or cheesecloth. Have an adult help you iron your paper between two clean rags if you want a smoother, flat surface.

Your paper is great for drawings, collages or prints with a textured background.

# MONSTER MUSH

Give new life to some mushy paper pulp by squishing, squeezing and piling together the parts of an amazing monster ... AHHHH! It's alive!!!

### Artist's Tools

- newspapers
- scrap paper
- bucket
- water
- wallpaper paste
- rubber gloves and stick for stirring (optional)
- plastic bag
- acrylic paint and paintbrushes
- fun finds (twigs, leavers, flowers, shells, stones, etc.)
- white glue

**1** Tear the scrap paper into pieces no bigger than the size of your palm.

**2** Working on a newspaper-covered surface, place the scraps into a bucket. Fill your bucket with enough water to wet your scraps well.

**3** Roll up your sleeves and, if you want, put on some rubber gloves. Add wallpaper paste to the mixture a little at a time and use a stick or your hands to mix it until it starts to look a little sticky. Add a little more water if the mixture gets too thick.

**4** Stir the gluey mixture thoroughly with your hand or a stick. Cover the top of your bucket with a plastic bag and let it sit for an hour or two or until your paper pulp mixture is nice and soft.

**5** Scoop out a handful of the mushy mixture from your bucket and squeeze it out a little. Be careful not to squeeze out too much paste, or your mushy monster might not hold its shape.

**6** Play with your mush as though it were very wet and squishy clay. Try

• pinching out some arms, legs or heads. How many of each does your monster have … two, four, ten?

• poking in some frightening facial features, such as eyes, ears, nose or mouth

• molding a big, round body

• flattening a base for big feet

**7** When you've finished shaping your paper-pulp monster, set it on the newspaper in a warm, dry spot. Let dry.

**8** Paint your monster with acrylic paint and glue on some fun finds such as shells, twigs, leaves, flowers and stones.

# AMAZING ANIMAL MASK

Capture the spirit of your
favorite animal by making
a mask that reflects what it
looks like from the inside out.

## Artist's Tools

- cloth
- self-hardening clay
- rolling pin (optional)
- plastic bowl or newspapers
- plastic knife
- white acrylic paint and paintbrush
- fun finds (branches, moss, bark, leaves, shells, vines, feathers, seeds, sand, etc.)
- glue gun and gloves
- twine or wire
- white glue
- strong string or leather cord

**1** Think about the type of animal that best represents your personality. A beautiful bird? A brave lion? A gentle deer? Research your animal by looking closely at its skull structure.

**2** On a cloth-covered work surface, flatten or roll out a ball of self-hardening clay into a large pancake shape. Make a small hole on two opposite sides of the flattened clay.

**3** Wrap the clay over a plastic bowl or a crumpled-up ball of newspaper. Cut and carve some skull-like features into the clay.

- eye sockets
- nostrils
- mouth

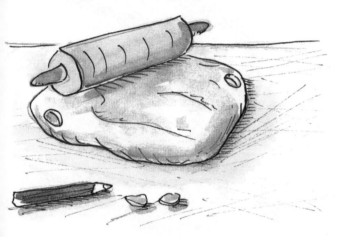

**4** Press on small pieces of clay to add more features. Teeth? Cheekbones? A beak? Small horns? Pinch all around the base of the pieces to make sure they stay on as they dry.

**5** Scratch in some textures before your skull mask dries.

**6** Let your mask dry and paint or stain it using watered-down acrylic paint or smudge on some chalk pastels.

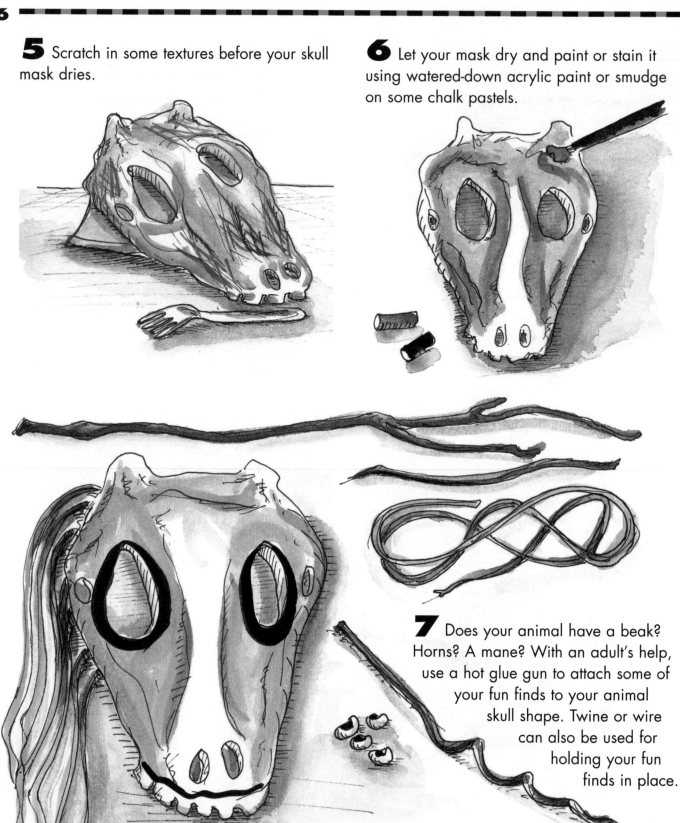

**7** Does your animal have a beak? Horns? A mane? With an adult's help, use a hot glue gun to attach some of your fun finds to your animal skull shape. Twine or wire can also be used for holding your fun finds in place.

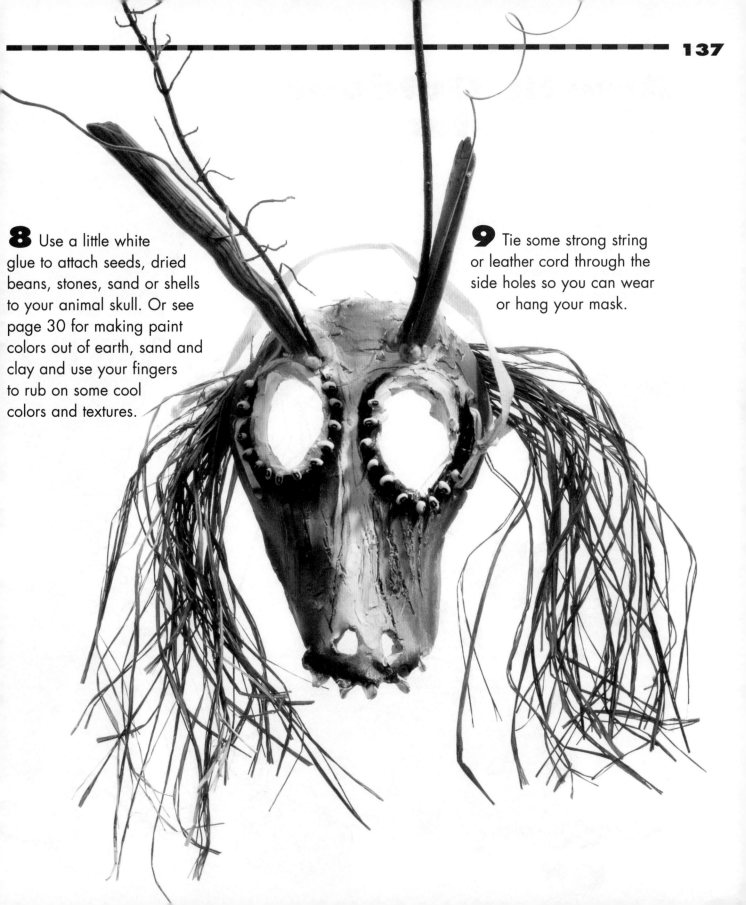

**8** Use a little white glue to attach seeds, dried beans, stones, sand or shells to your animal skull. Or see page 30 for making paint colors out of earth, sand and clay and use your fingers to rub on some cool colors and textures.

**9** Tie some strong string or leather cord through the side holes so you can wear or hang your mask.

# Artistic Outdoor Observatory

Create your own wild
kingdom in your room, on
your balcony or in your yard.
It's a great way to go to
make sure you never run
out of outdoor
art ideas.

# The Avenue Road Arts School Artists

The Avenue Road Arts School was founded in Toronto, Canada, in 1993. It's a place where everyone can become an artistic adventurer and where making art — all kinds of art — is a great way to discover your many hidden talents and a soaring imagination.

As your guides, we want every artistic adventurer to be excited about taking those natural steps toward artistic discovery. That's why the activities in this book reflect both a playful attitude that we think makes learning fun and the experience and know-how of the artists who have traveled before us.

After taking this outdoor art adventure with us, we hope that you have found your creative confidence and discovered that you really can draw, paint, sculpt and build a wild and wonderful world!

This book would not be possible without the inspiring work and ideas of the following Avenue Road Arts School artist–instructors

**Jennifer Chin** for her work regarding Sundial-Inspired Assemblage (pages 102–3) and for her ideas for creating Silly Silhouettes (page 99).

**Taggett Cornish** for her thoughts and ideas on cloud watching and lightning strikes that inspired Searching the Sky (pages 104–7) and for her suggestions regarding the artful decomposition of leaves and natural fabrics that led to Artful Aging (page 128).

**Liana Del Mastro Vicente** for her idea for Super Spider's Web (pages 64–65) and for her ideas regarding making music with nature, making an excursion journal and using natural shapes in art.

**Madeleine Dominigue** for her thoughts on crop circles that inspired Silly Sprouts (pages 48–49).

**Julie Frost** for her studio lesson A Slice of Life, which contributed to Layered Landscape (pages 12–13) and for her suggestions for Solar-Powered Prints (page 100–101). Thanks also for her inspiring studio lessons Paper Bag Stories, Casting Nature's Wonders, Birds-Eye Maps and See-Through Nature.

**Julie Galloway** for her project idea Layer upon Layer, which contributed to Layered Landscape (pages 12–13) and for her ideas regarding pressed plants and flowers (pages 58–59). Thanks also for her idea for Rainy Day Symphony, which became a part of Great Flowing Fountain (pages 90–93).

**Martha Johnson** for her ideas for Woven Wonders (pages 62–63).

**Joni Moriyama** for her ideas regarding frozen ice sculptures and Sparkling Ice Chandelier (page 96–98).

**Linda Prussick** for her ideas for Terrific Topiaries (page 50–51), Frozen Patterned Paper (page 95) and Great Flowing Fountain (pages 90–93).

**Julianne Trewartha** for her thoughts on nature's repeating patterns, which inspired the colors and drawings used in Beautiful Batik (pages 54–55).

**Susie Whaley** for her project ideas Surprise Garden and Tree Stenciling, which led to Secret Garden (page 46–47).

# GLOSSARY

**Art**
Creative thought expressed as drawing, painting, sculpture, music, movement or writing.

**Assemblage**
A sculpture made of a variety of materials, such as scraps of wood, cloth, string, cardboard and metal.

**Asymmetrical**
A word used to describe an object or image that has two different or unbalanced sides. The opposite of symmetrical.

**Balance**
Parts of art, such as its lines, shapes and forms, arranged to have equal weight.

**Batik**
An Indonesian technique for artfully dyeing fabric. A design or pattern is drawn on fabric using wax. When the fabric is dyed, the design or pattern stays the original color of the fabric.

**Botanical**
A word used to describe plants or plant life. Detailed drawings or paintings of plants are often called botanical studies.

**Carving**
Cutting a figure or design into wood, clay or other solid materials.

**Collage**
A composition made from a variety of 2-dimensional materials, such as homemade paper, magazine clippings and dried leaves.

**Composition**
An element of design that refers to how different parts of art are arranged or placed to form a whole.

**Contrast**
Opposites arranged beside or close to each other in a composition to show their differences. Blue and orange are examples of contrasting colors.

**Dimension**
The measurement of an object's height, width or depth. Flat objects have 2 dimensions (height and width) and objects with volume have 3 dimensions (height, width and depth).

**Diorama**
A miniature, 3-dimensional sculpture made to look like a tiny scene.

**Earthenware**
Clay dishes such as plates, jugs, cups or vases.

**Form**
The shape of a 3-dimensional object.

**Highlight**
A bright spot added to a drawn or painted object in order to make it 3-dimensional.

**Horizon**
The line where the earth and sky seem to meet.

**Installation**
A drawing, painting, sculpture or mixed-media work of art made for a particular space or room.

**Landscape**
A scene or view of the outdoors.

### Line
A continuous straight or curved mark. Lines can be 2-dimensional (for example, one made with a pencil mark on paper) or 3-dimensional (for example, one made with a piece of wire).

### Mixed Media
Art made using a combination of tools, materials and techniques.

### Modeling
Shaping or forming material into art.

### Opaque
The dark or dull appearance of a finish, such as paint, that light cannot pass through.

### Organic
Material that comes from plants or animals. Organic objects look like shapes found in nature or living things.

### Perspective
The way artists create the feeling of 3 dimensions on a flat surface such as a drawing or painting.

### Pigment
The ingredient that gives paint its color.

### Primary Colors
The colors red, blue and yellow. Primary colors cannot be made by mixing other colors.

### Print
A mark or design made on a surface by adding pressure. The image left behind after pressing paint-covered leaves or flowers onto a paper surface is a type of print.

### Sculpture
A work of art that is 3-dimensional, such as a wooden figure or a mobile.

### Shading
The dark lines, marks or smudges used to fill in a sketch or drawing.

### Shadow box
A deep frame for displaying art or collected objects.

### Shape
The definite form of an object or image. Rectangles, squares, cylinders, triangles, etc., are all common shapes.

### Secondary Colors
Colors made by mixing primary colors. Orange, green and violet are secondary colors.

### Silhouette
A solid image made to look like the outline of an object or person.

### Still life
An arrangement of unmoving objects drawn, painted or recreated by an artist.

### Symmetrical
A word used to describe an object or image that has two even or balanced sides. The opposite of asymmetrical.

### Texture
How rough or smooth something feels or looks like it feels.

### Topiary
A tree or bush trimmed in a decorative style. For example, topiaries can be made to look like animals, birds or geometric shapes.

### Transparent
The see-through appearance of a finish, such as paint, as the light passes through it.

### Weaving
A technique that involves passing strips of material under and over other strips of material to make a flat surface or fabric.

# INDEX